The Masonic Book Club

Vol. 8A

Trestle-Board

Baltimore Masonic Convention

Foreword by Dwight L. Smith

Westphalia Press
An Imprint of the Policy Studies Organization
Washington, DC

TRESTLE-BOARD

All Rights Reserved © 2025 by Policy Studies Organization

Westphalia Press
An imprint of Policy Studies Organization
1367 Connecticut Avenue NW
Washington, D.C. 20036
info@ipsonet.org

ISBN: 978-1-63723-563-8

Daniel Gutierrez-Sandoval, Executive Director
PSO and Westphalia Press

Updated material and comments on this edition
can be found at the Westphalia Press website:
www.westphaliapress.org

THE MASONIC BOOK CLUB

The *Masonic Book Club* (MBC) was formed in 1970 by two Illinois Masons, Alphonse Cerza, 33°, and Louis L. Williams, 33°. The MBC primarily reprinted out-of-print Masonic books with scholarly introductions; occasionally they would print additional texts as "bonuses" (though none were marked specifically as such on the title pages); sometimes a reprint would be marked "Masonic Book Club Edition"; often an unnumbered bonus was published jointly with the Illinois Lodge of Research or the Supreme Council, 33°, NMJ, USA.

Most of the MBC volumes indicated on the title page, "Volume [*Number*] of the Publications of the Masonic Book Club," some were misnumbered, and some were unnumbered. Indeed, the numbering of the early volumes was inconsistent. For example, *A Serious and Impartial Enquiry* is "Volume Five" (1974) but *Masonic Membership of the Founding Fathers* is "The Masonic Book Club Edition" (1974). Then, *Masonry Dissected* is "Volume Eight" (1977), *The Trestleboard* is "Volume 8A" (1978), and *Anderson's Constitutions of 1738* is "Volume Nine" (1978). If nothing else, MBC books keep bibliophiles on their toes.

The first volumes had deckle-edged paper and pages of slightly different sizes, though eventually the MBC settled into a 6″×9″ trimmed-page format for their books. The books were bound in a dark blue fabric with gold lettering. Listed below are the fifty-nine MBC volumes published 1970–2010 with bonuses. N.B.: A number and letter, e.g. "Volume 8A," is a numbering for this reprint series.

The club originally was limited to 333 members, but the number grew to nearly 2,000, with 1,083 members when it dissolved in 2010. In 2017 MW Barry Weer, 33°, the last president of the MBC, transferred the MBC name and assets to the Supreme Council, 33°, SJ, USA. Under the editorship of Arturo de Hoyos, 33°, G∴C∴, and S. Brent Morris, 33°, G∴C∴, the revived Masonic Book Club has the goal of publishing classic Masonic books while supporting Scottish Rite, SJ, USA philanthropies.

Publications of the Masonic Book Club, 1970–2010

1	1970	*The Regius Poem*	Masonic Book Club
2	1971	*The Constitutions of the Free-Masons*	Benjamin Franklin
3	1972	*Ahiman Rezon*	Laurence Dermott
4	1973	*Illustrations of Masonry*	William Preston
5	1974	*A Serious and Impartial Enquiry into the Cause of the Present Decay of Free-Masonry in the Kingdom of Ireland*	Fifield D'Assigny
5A	1974*	*Masonic Membership of the Founding Fathers*	Ronald E. Heaton

6	1975	*The Signers of the Declaration of Independence*	David C. Whitney
7	1976	*The Signers of the Constitution of the United States*	David C. Whitney
7A	1976*	*Masonic Symbols in American Decorative Art*	Louis L. Williams & Alphonse Cerza
8	1977	*Samuel Prichard's Masonry Dissected, 1730*	Harry Carr
8A	1978*	*Trestle-Board (A facsimile of the original Trestle Board by the Baltimore Masonic Convention of 1843)*	Dwight L. Smith
9	1978	*Anderson's Constitutions of 1738*	Lewis Edward & W. J. Hughan
10	1979	*Sufferings of John Coustos*	Wallace McLeod
11	1980	*The Revelations of a Square*	George Oliver
11A	1980	*Biblical Characters in Freemasonry*	John H. Van Gorden
11B	1980*	*A Masonic Reader's Guide*	*Guide* Alphonse Cerza & Thomas Warden
12	1981	*Three Distinct Knocks and Jachin and Boaz*	Harry Carr
13	1982	*Masonic Almanacs and Anti-Masonic Almanacs*	Plez A. Transou
13A	1982*	*Stephen A. Douglas: Freemason*	Wayne C. Temple
14	1983	*The Beginnings of Freemasonry in America*	Melvin M. Johnson
14A	1983*	*Bespangled, Painted & Embroidered: Decorated Masonic Aprons in America, 1790–1850*	Scottish Rite Masonic Museum & Library
14B	1983*	*Making a Mason at Sight*	Louis L. Williams
15	1984	*Masonic Concordance of the Holy Bible*	Charles Clyde Hunt
15A	1984*	*By Square and Compasses: The Building of Lincoln's Home and Its Saga*	Wayne C. Temple

16	1985	*The Old Gothic Constitutions*	Wallace McLeod
16A	1985*	*Modern Historical Characters in Freemasonry*	John H. Van Gorden
17	1986	*The Rise and Development of Organised Freemasonry*	Roy A. Wells
17A	1986*	*Ancient and Early Medieval Historical Characters in Freemasonry*	John H. Van Gorden
18	1987	*The Lodge in Friendship Village and Other Stories*	P. W. George
18A	1987*	*Masonic Charities*	John H. Van Gorden & Stewart M. L. Pollard
18B	1987*	*Medieval Historical Characters in Freemasonry*	John H. Van Gorden
18C	1987*	*George Washington in New York*	Allan Boudreau & Alexander Bleimann
19	1988	*Records of the Hole Crafte and Fellowship of Masons*	Edward Conder, Jr.
20	1989	*A Candid Disquisition of the Principles and Practices of the Most Ancient and Honourable Society of Free and Accepted Masons*	Wellins Calcott
20A	1989*	*Freemasonry and Nauvoo, 1839–1846*	Robin L. Carr
21	1990	*Masonic Odes and Poems*	Rob Morris
22	1991	*Lessing's Masonic Dialogues*	Gotthold Lessing
22A	1991*	*ABC of Freemasonry: A Book for Beginners*	Delmar D. Darrah
23	1992	*The Folger Manuscript*	S. Brent Morris
24	1993	*Freemasonry and Christianity: Lectures from Two Ages*	T. De Witt Peake & John J. Murchison
25	1994	*The Constitutions of St. John's Lodge*	Robin L. Carr
25A	1994*	*The Mystic Tie and Men of Letters*	Robin L. Carr
26	1995	*Recollections of a Masonic Veteran*	S. Brent Morris

27	1996	*The Freemason's Monitor or Illustrations of Masonry in Two Parts*	Thomas Smith Webb
28	1997	*The Masonic Ladder or the Nine Steps to Ancient Freemasonry*	John Sherer
28A	1997*	*Freemasonry and Democracy: Its Evolution in North America*	Allen E. Roberts & Wallace McLeod
29	1998	*The Masonic Harp: Collection of Masonic Odes, Hymns, Songs*	George Wingate Chase
30	1999	*Symbolic Teachings of Masonry and Its Message*	Thomas Milton Stewart
31	2000	*Freemasonry Its Meaning and Significance, An Exposition of its Ethics, Religion and Philosophy*	Otto Caspari
32	2001	*K. R. Cama Masonic Jubilee Volume*	Jivanji Jamshedji Modi
33	2002	*Caementaria Hibernica*	W. J. Chetwode Crawley
34	2003	*A Daily Advancement in Masonic Knowledge*	Wallace McLeod & S. Brent Morris
35	2004	*The Craftsman, and Templar's Textbook and, also, Melodies for the Craft*	Cornelius Moore
36	2005	*The Text Book of Freemasonry*	Retired Member of the Craft
37	2006	*Orations of the Illustrious Brother Frederick Dalcho Esq., M.D.*	Frederick Dalcho
38	2007	*Antiquities of Freemasonry Comprising Illustrations of the Five Grand Periods of Masonry from the Creation of the World to the Dedication of King Solomon's Temple*	George Oliver
39	2008	*Diogenes' Lamp or an Examination of our Present-Day Morality and Enlightenment*	Adam Weishaupt
40	2009	*Proofs of Conspiracy Against All the Governments of Europe*	John Robison
41	2010	*The Evolution of Freemasonry*	Delmar Darrah

*indicates a bonus book

TRESTLE-BOARD

Trestle-Board

Trestle-Board

A facsimile reprint of the original

Trestle-Board

published by the

Baltimore Masonic Convention

of 1843

with foreword by

Dwight L. Smith, P.G.M., Grand Secretary

Grand Lodge F. & A.M. of Indiana

Volume 8A

of the publications of

The Masonic Book Club

Published by

The Masonic Book Club

A Not-for-Profit Corporation of Illinois

Bloomington, Illinois

1978

[This text appeared in the original publication.]

This volume has been published
for Members of
The Masonic Book Club
in an edition of 1,200 copies
numbered for members of the Club
this being

No. 407

© 1978 by The Masonic Book Club
Printed in the United States of America

Preface

The National Masonic Congress which met in Baltimore, Maryland on May 8, 1843 and remained in session for nine days is an important event in the history of Freemasonry in the United States. The professed purpose of the meeting was to bring about a uniformity of the Masonic ritual in the United States and to recommend to the Grand Lodges matters that would be beneficial to the Craft.

What happened at the Congress is of general interest for a number of reasons. Since the ritual is transmitted orally and in the early days of the development of the Craft there were no written Monitors, differences in the ritual from place to place is to be expected. The fact that the Congress was held is an indication that some members are of the belief that uniformity in the ritual is desirable. If nothing tangible was accomplished at the meeting, the Congress, at least, created an awareness of the problem and that probably something ought to be done about the matter. Prior and subsequent such conferences seem to indicate that no uniformity will ever be accomplished, however.

The second matter considered by the Congress was the attempt to form a permanent national organization of all the Grand Lodges in the United States with meetings to be held each three years. Nothing came of this phase of the discussion because of the inherent fear that such a group would lead to the formation of a General Grand Lodge of the United States. Suggestions along this line have always been met with strong opposition.

One benefit brought about by the Congress was the creation and encouragement of traveling teachers or lecturers of the Masonic ritual. Many Grand Lodges appointed Lecturers who traveled about the state teaching the ritual to lodge officers. There were also a number of Masonic Lecturers who traveled around the country demonstrating and teaching the work. There was a real need for their services as the Craft emerged from the devastating effects of the anti-Masonic era that came into full bloom with the William Morgan disappearance. These traveling Lecturers created some degree of uniformity in the ritual.

The printing of various Masonic Monitors and their wide circulation also helped create a degree of uniformity in the work. It is worthy of note that in England there is no standard ritual. There are about half a dozen popular forms of the ritual used in England and each lodge selects its own form. Brother Harry Carr, one of the world's outstanding Masonic scholars, who is an authority on the history of the Masonic ritual, has stated in his excellent book "The Freemason at Work," that "The United Grand Lodge of England does not publish, nor does it give its authorization to any specific form of ritual, either written, printed or spoken." (Page 47). It is to be observed that changes in the ritual have taken place with the passage of time. For example, it was not until about the year 1725 that a third degree was made a part of the degrees conferred in a Masonic Lodge. And it is to be noted that in the early 1960's the United Grand Lodge of England gave serious consideration to the changing of the penalties contained in the work and the result was that lodges were given the choice of continuing their use, or to substitute a mere reference to the ancient penalties. These two instances are noted as illustrations of how there can be a lack of uniformity in the Masonic ritual from place to place.

Whether there should be uniformity is a matter of serious debate. It is sometimes urged that uniformity is desirable because of the claimed universality of the Craft and also to make it easier for traveling Masons to identify themselves and to also feel at home. On the other hand, it is sometimes urged that variations make for interest as one visits lodges from place to place. It is a continuing friendly debate that will never be solved.

When Brother Dwight L. Smith, Grand Secretary, and a Past Grand Master of the State of Indiana, recommended to your officers that our Book Club reproduce the "Trestle Board" which describes the Baltimore Convention, it was easy to decide to publish the book for our members. The volume meets the established objectives of the Club to make available to its members Masonic classics that are out-of-print. Since the Club had some surplus funds the volume is being prepared and sent to our members as a "bonus book in the year 1978." Since Brother Smith is a skilled researcher and writer he was invited to write an Introduction for this volume. He has done an excellent job in placing the volume in proper perspective in the light of Masonic history. On behalf of all our members we thank him for the suggestion he made as well as his writing of the brilliant Introduction.

On behalf of all our members we also thank Brother Robert P. Beach, Grand Secretary of the Grand Lodge of Massachusetts, who graciously loaned us the original copy of the "Trestle-Board" which was in the Grand Lodge of Massachusetts Library in Boston. We were thus enabled to reproduce a facsimile copy of this book.

We direct your attention to the text of the Circular appearing at the end of the facsimile itself. This is one of the most interesting developments of the convention. Brother Moore, Grand Secretary of Massachusetts, had a disagreement with Brother Dove, Grand Secretary of Virginia, and this story is told in the Circular. It is the most interesting part of the whole volume, and is a very rare item, with perhaps no more than a half dozen copies surviving.

ALPHONSE CERZA
LOUIS L. WILLIAMS

Table of Contents

FOREWORD xi

FACSIMILE REPRODUCTION OF TRESTLE-BOARD xvii

REPRODUCTION OF (CIRCULAR) 89

COLOPHON 110

Foreword

One of the oddities of American Freemasonry is the persistence of a conviction that Masonic ritual should be everywhere the same, right down to the last word. In a nation of rebellious tendencies where diversity is looked upon with favor in almost every other area, such a philosophy would seem to be out of character for Americans. Furthermore, a uniform system is not consistent historically with the traditions of the Craft. As Henry Wilson Coil observes, "No great inconvenience exists by reason of diversity, and no particular benefits would flow from absolute unification."

But our forefathers thought otherwise. Efforts at uniformity through Conventions or Congresses began as early as 1822 and continued from time to time until 1893.

To understand how it all came about, we must delve into the background of ritual in England. Originally, the admission ceremony of the operative Masons consisted of little more than an obligation of secrecy, supplemented in the course of time by a few more or less "standard" questions and answers. Those questions and answers recur regularly as a kind of nucleus of the catechisms in the later and fuller versions of the 18th Century.

Our earliest ritual documents begin in 1696 with a description of the two degrees of that period, and throughout the seventeen hundreds, with the emergence of the system of three degrees, we can trace in the successive texts the expansion of the catechisms to include details of the officers, their situation and duties, the tools, jewels, furniture and their symbolism. In effect, we are able to watch the growth of the basic material in the lectures on the three degrees of Masonry. Each version added to their verbosity and some of the later revisions, unfortunately, changed the meaning of the lessons the original lectures sought to convey.

It must be remembered also that in the United States we did not receive our work from one source, but from several; nor did we obtain it as a whole. The early Lodges established in the colonies had charters from two Grand Lodges in England, from Ireland, from Scotland, and from France, each with its own system of working and none with a uniform ritual, so that to this day our American work sometimes leans to one, sometimes to another, and more often to more than one.

Greatest of all the expounders of the ritual was William Preston, in whose *Illustrations of Masonry*, 1772, with many enlarged editions from 1775 onwards, followed later by his lectures on the first, second and third degree of Masonry, may be found the basic sources for the lectures in most American Jurisdictions, though in greatly condensed form.

Preston's work was used widely in England until 1813, when the United Grand Lodge adopted the Hemming revisions, which were based substantially on a rearrangement of Preston's material. But by that time Freemasonry was firmly established on American soil. Communication was slow, indeed oftentimes non-existent, so that if our Brethren on this side of the Atlantic knew anything about the changes of 1813, they paid no attention to the news from overseas, for they were already at work. As early as 1797 Thomas Smith Webb, a New Englander, had copied the Preston lectures and published his own version. To a great extent Webb's version became the American work, remaining so during the early part of the 19th Century with little or no alteration.

All too soon the Fraternity in the United States was threatened with extinction because of anti-Masonic agitation which had assumed a decidedly hostile attitude by 1798. Itinerant preachers and circuit riders began denouncing Freemasonry, publishing their booklets and tracts for at least 20 years before the notorious Morgan affair in 1826. To combat so-called exposures, alterations were made in various portions of the esoteric work. Examining committees were prone to adopt an air of suspicion whenever a sojourner sought to visit a Lodge. Lack of uniformity became not only an obstacle between Lodges of different Jurisdictions, but oftentimes between Lodges in the same State.

Largely because of such chaotic conditions, leaders of the Craft sought means of unification through Conventions of Grand Lodges. Most notable of these was that which met at Baltimore May 8-17, 1843.

The Grand Lodge of Alabama in 1839 had advanced a proposal that each Grand Lodge elect a delegate to meet in Washington, D.C., in March 1842 "for the purpose of determining a uniform form of work throughout all the Lodges in the United States." A two-day meeting was held, but with only 11 Jurisdictions participating. Little was accomplished other than the adoption of a resolution introduced by Grand Secretary Charles W. Moore of Massachusetts that each Grand Lodge elect a Grand Lecturer, and that the officials thus chosen convene in Baltimore on the second Monday in May, 1843, to exemplify and, if possible, approve a specific working to become the standard ritual for the three degrees.

Only half of the 28 Jurisdictions then operating in the United States accepted the invitation. On the second day the delegates adopted a statement declaring their objectives to be twofold: "To produce uniformity of Masonic work" and "To recommend such measures as shall tend to the elevation of this Order to its due degree of respect throughout the world at large."

With few exceptions, the delegates found themselves in agreement to an extraordinary degree while in Baltimore. But after going home it was found that they were in almost total disagreement as to what had happened. And when the work of the Convention (or what they thought it to have been) was set forth by Charles W. Moore, of Massachusetts, and S. W. B. Carnegy, of Missouri, in *The New Masonic Trestle-Board*, it was found to be at variance with that of another monitor prepared by John Dove, of Virginia, presumably from the same source material. Some idea of the vigor with which the running battle between Brothers Moore and Dove was conducted may be seen in the Moore circular which is made a part of this reproduction.

Be that as it may, the Convention's work was widely respected. Eventually most or all of its recommendations were adopted by American Jurisdictions. It fell short of its goal, that of unifying ritualistic work, but it made certain significant contributions. They were four in number:

1. Due Guards and Signs. Not until about the close of the 18th Century were due guards and signs distinguished as such. Usually the expression due guard and sign were used interchangeably as designating the same thing.

Before the American Revolution, the Entered Apprentice sign was known as the due guard *or* sign. Due guards of both the Entered Apprentice and Fellow Craft degrees were unknown, or at least were not used as such. Thus, the Entered Apprentice and Fellow Craft degrees had one sign only.

By 1800, in the Entered Apprentice degree, what is now the due guard was termed the sign, and what is now the sign was called the due guard. The Baltimore Convention reversed these.

In the Fellow Craft degree, both due guard and sign were given in about the same manner as now. The Convention left this practice unchanged.

The due guard in the Master Mason degree was given with the right hand only. The Convention recommended the use of both hands.

2. Movable and Immovable Jewels. The old system used in England termed the immovable jewels of a Lodge the Rough Ashlar, the Perfect Ashlar, and the Trestle Board. The Baltimore Convention recommended that in American Lodges these be termed *movable* jewels, and that the immovable jewels be the Square, the Level, and the Plumb.

Charles W. Moore's *Freemason's Monthly Magazine*, published at Boston, explained the Convention's reasoning in 1847: "They (the Plumb, Square, and Level) are the permanent and unchangeable jewels of the Lodge, and can never be taken or removed from their proper place, to be worn by officers of inferior rank, or who are acting in any other capacities than those indicated by the jewels. They belong permanently and immovably to the three principal chairs or offices."

3. Business of Lodge in Master Mason Degree. Traditionally, the business of a Lodge was conducted in a Lodge of Entered Apprentices, a practice that remains today in many parts of the world. When the Baltimore Convention recommended that business be transacted only in the Master Mason degree, it was devising yet another scheme to ward off imposters and be added to the relics of the anti-Masonic era.

In many old monitors and on many early wall charts used for delivering the lectures may be seen crude representations of the Mosaic Pavement, the Middle Chamber, and the Sanctum Sanctorum. In connection with these sketches appear the cryptic figures:

$$7\frac{1}{6} \qquad 5\frac{2}{3} \qquad 3$$

Several years ago, with the help of an old exposé, I learned the meaning of the drawings and their accompanying numbers. It was a bit of imaginary nonsense in the third section of the lecture of the Master Mason degree, advanced in an effort to make it appear that ancient tradition supported the practice of conducting Lodge business in the Master Mason degree only.

According to the old lecture, a Lodge of Entered Apprentices must consist of one Master Mason and six Entered Apprentices, a total of seven (hence, $7\frac{1}{6}$). Fellow Crafts had to have five in order to meet, two Master Masons and three Fellow Crafts, total five (hence, $5\frac{2}{3}$). But Master Masons required only three (hence, the figure 3).

Most American monitors published a century ago contained this material with its explanation of how Fellow Crafts, presumably all 80,000 of them, met in the Middle Chamber "on the evening of the sixth day to receive their wages." Few, if any, have it now.

4. Religious Universality. Perhaps the most significant recommendation of the Baltimore Convention was that which urged American Grand Lodges to eliminate a reference in the Entered Apprentice lecture to the Blazing Star

as commemorative of the Star of Bethlehem. Even in 1843 when Christianity was, in effect, considered to be the "established religion" of American Freemasonry despite the first of the Old Charges, the Convention delegates were perceptive enough to know that Freemasonry's non-sectarianism was one of its greatest assets, and that therefore, the Christian reference to the Wise Men of the East and to "the place of our Saviour's nativity" should be deleted.

It took a long time for Jurisdictions in the United States to agree to a practical application of that universality of which we boast, but as of this date, all have omitted the Star of Bethlehem explanation except three.

Thus, the Baltimore Convention did indeed make a modest contribution to the development and the maturing of Freemasonry in the United States. True, its steps were feeble, but they were steps. In reproducing the 1843 *Trestle-Board*, The Masonic Book Club is hopeful that another rare work of historical value may be made available to an increasing number of students seeking further light on that important period in our history.

Dwight L. Smith

February 3, 1978

FACSIMILE PAGES
of
TRESTLE-BOARD

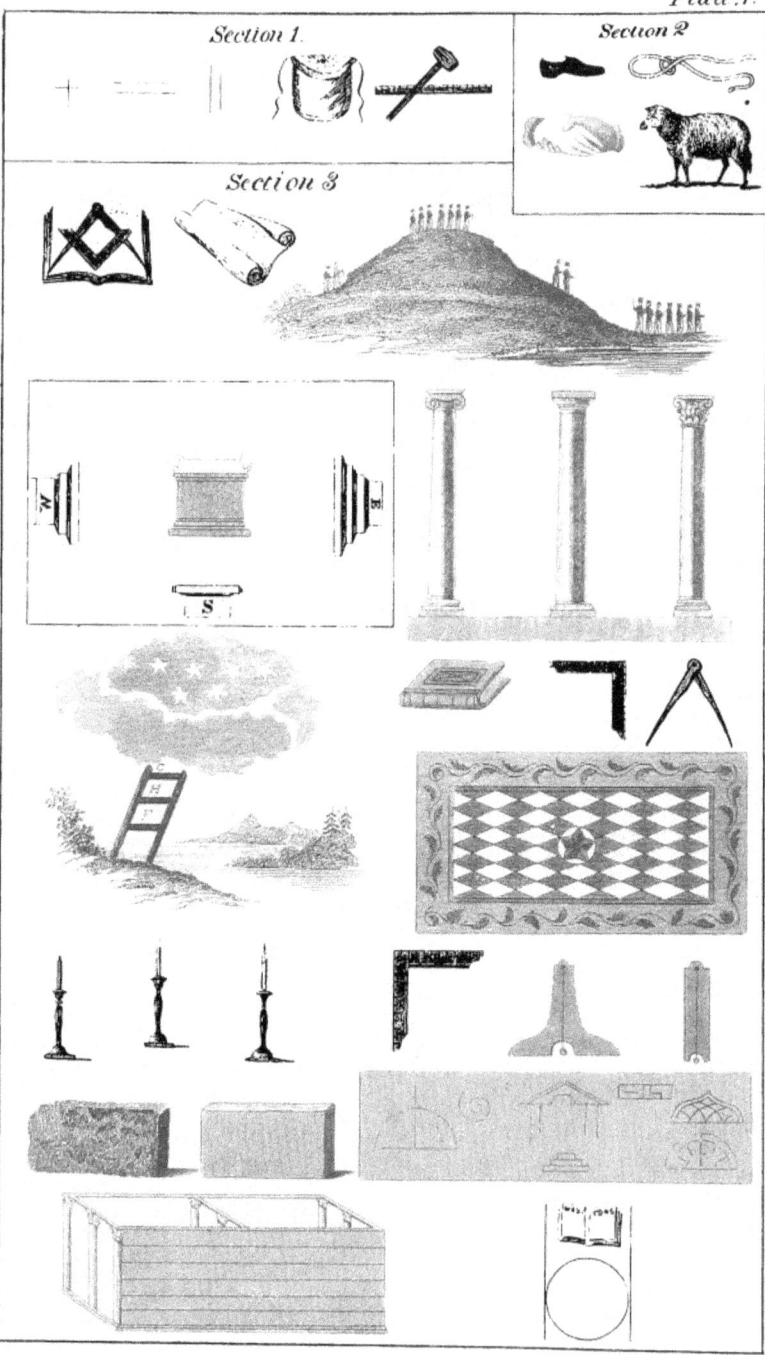

THE

MASONIC TRESTLE-BOARD,

ADAPTED TO THE

NATIONAL SYSTEM OF WORK AND LECTURES,

AS

REVISED AND PERFECTED

BY THE

UNITED STATES MASONIC CONVENTION,

AT

BALTIMORE, MARYLAND, A. L. 5843.

BY CHARLES W. MOORE & S. W. B. CARNEGY,

MAJORITY OF THE COMMITTEE APPOINTED BY THE CONVENTION TO PREPARE THE WORK.

BOSTON:
PUBLISHED BY CHARLES W. MOORE,
21 SCHOOL STREET.
TUTTLE & DENNETT, PRINTERS.
1843.

Entered according to Act of Congress, in the year 1843,
By CHARLES W. MOORE,
In the Clerk's Office of the District Court of Massachusetts.

RECOMMENDATIONS.

We, the subscribers, officers of the M. W. Grand Lodge of Massachusetts, unite in the approval of the "TRESTLE-BOARD," prepared by R. W. Brothers MOORE and CARNEGY, agreeably to a vote of the late National Masonic Convention, for the general use of the Lodges in the United States. It contains all that is proper and essential to a correct understanding of every thing pertaining to a Lodge. Its arrangement evinces a sound discrimination and a matured judgment on matters important to the Craft; and it embraces the true interpretation of ancient Craft Masonry. Its peculiar adaptation as a *working book*, with the beautiful and aptly arranged FLOORINGS, give to the work a decided preference over any other hitherto published which we have seen. We, therefore, most cordially give it the sanction of our names, and recommend it to the general patronage of the Lodges.

AUGUSTUS PEABODY, G. M.   WINSLOW LEWIS, J. G. W.
S. W. ROBINSON, D. G. M.   JOHN J. LORING, G. Treas.
THOMAS TOLMAN, S. G. W.   WINSLOW LEWIS, Jr., Cor. G. Sec.

EAST-CAMBRIDGE, Nov. 25, 1843.

Brother C. W. MOORE—

Dear Sir—Having, at your request, examined the new "TRESTLE-BOARD," prepared by you and Brother CARNEGY, for the use and benefit of the United States Lodges, it is with much satisfaction that I bear testimony to its merits, and hereby cordially recommend it to the patronage of the Fraternity, " wherever dispersed," as a *correct* and *useful Manual*—better adapted to the purposes designed, than other more extensive and expensive publications.

It was my privilege, while at Brown University, Providence, R. I., (1801-2,) to acquire a complete knowledge of the Lectures in the *three* first degrees of Masonry, *directly* from our late much esteemed Br. THOS. S. WEBB, author of the Freemasons' Monitor; and, in consequence, was appointed and commissioned, by the Grand Lodge of Massachusetts and Maine, Grand Lecturer, devoting the whole time to the instruction of the Lodges under the jurisdiction,—and for many years subsequently, (as Professor of Astronomy and Geography,) visiting all the different States in the Union, and (1829-30) many parts of Europe—successfully communicating, to numerous Lodges and Associations of Brethren, these same valuable " Lectures of the Craft"—according to the " ancient landmarks." Wherefore, as a Brother " well instructed," permit me, without hesitation, earnestly to recommend your *good work*, as well calculated to facilitate the acquisition of the Lectures,—to preserve the ceremonials and usages, traditions and lectures, in their purity, and to encourage and ensure a *general uniformity* among the Brotherhood throughout our " community of interests," in our " ancient and honorable" Profession.

Respectfully, your Friend and Brother,   BENJAMIN GLEASON.

BOSTON, Nov. 27, 1843.

Having examined " THE TRESTLE-BOARD," with some care, I cheerfully record my testimony to the excellent service which R. W. CHARLES W. MOORE and R. W. STEPHEN W. B. CARNEGY have done to the Fraternity, in its successful completion. It is concise, perspicuous, and free from the unnecessary Masonic literature which has encumbered similar works. Its great excellence, and what should recommend it to the approval of all good Masons, is the *practical purpose of every page.*

THOMAS POWER, *P. G. Sec. of the G. Lodge of Mass.*

R. W. BR. MOORE:

I have examined the new "TRESTLE-BOARD," prepared by you and R. W. Br. Carnegy, (being a majority of the Committee appointed for the purpose by the late Masonic Convention,) with great satisfaction. I have been an active Mason for forty-three years, have sustained the office of S. G. W. of the Grand Lodge of Massachusetts; was D. D. Grand Master under the Grand Lodge of Virginia; Deputy Grand Master, and for three years Grand Lecturer for the Grand Lodge of the District of Columbia, and have several times presided as Master of subordinate Lodges. I have therefore necessarily been led to make myself fully acquainted with all the principal text-books which have from time to time been given to the Fraternity, and I most cordially and unequivocally recommend the Trestle-Board as being more practical and better adapted to Lodge purposes, than any other work which has fallen under my observation.   JOHN B. HAMMATT.

BOSTON, DEC. 5, 1843.

The undersigned, having carefully examined the new MASONIC TRESTLE-BOARD, prepared by Brs. MOORE and CARNEGY, cheerfully recommend it to the Lodges and Brethren generally, as a work peculiarly well adapted to facilitate the acquisition of a correct and thorough knowledge of the various and important duties which devolve upon the active members of every Lodge, but more especially upon those filling responsible official stations. In its arrangement and execution it is, in our judgment, superior to any similar work with which we are acquainted; and we cannot doubt

RECOMMENDATIONS.

that it will be an important agent in establishing that degree of *uniformity*, which is essential to the perpetuity and prosperity of our ancient Institution. We, therefore, cordially recommend it to the patronage of the Fraternity throughout the country.

GILBERT NURSE, D. D. G. Master,
JOHN R. BRADFORD, G. Marshal,
And Grand Lecturers of the Grand Lodge of Massachusetts.

The undersigned, Members of the late National Masonic Convention, having examined the TRESTLE-BOARD, prepared by R. W. Brs. MOORE and CARNEGY, recommend it to the Fraternity throughout the United States, as a MANUAL, singularly well adapted to the purpose for which its publication was ordered by the Convention. They believe that its general use by the Lodges will greatly tend to ensure uniformity in the Work and Lectures.

ALBERT CASE, of South Carolina.
JOHN H. WHEELER, of North Carolina.
JOSEPH FOSTER, of Missouri.
THOMAS CLAPHAM, of New-Hampshire.
WILLIAM FIELD, of Rhode Island.
DANIEL A. PIPER, of Maryland.
THOMAS HAYWARD, of Florida.

"*Charleston, S. C., Dec.* 1843.

R. W. Br. MOORE,—I have received and carefully examined the new "MASONIC TRESTLE-BOARD," prepared by yourself and P. G. M. Carnegy, in accordance with the will of the National Masonic Convention. I congratulate the Editors on the completion of their labors, and while I regret that the Committee were not entirely unanimous in presenting so invaluable a work, I assure you that, in my opinion, the "TRESTLE-BOARD" *is all the Convention desired it should be*—better than any other text-book for Masonic purposes and that it will meet the approbation of the Convention, and the Fraternity. The omission suggested by the dissenting Brother, would much lessen the value of the work for general use. To the exoteric Mason the omission would be no disadvantage. But there are, and will be many of the esoteric school, who rule in Lodges, and to such, the illustrations are absolutely necessary. If the text-book did not contain them, the Master and Pupil would often be found far in the *North*, seeking knowledge in the dark.

I repeat—I believe the book is what the Convention desired; that it will be of infinite service in securing uniformity in the work of the Lodges, and that the intelligent craftsmen, who have prepared it, will see their work approved, and be greeted by the Convention with "well done," faithful and true Brothers. ALBERT CASE,
Sec. of the late Nat. Masonic Convention."

We, the subscribers, officers of the M. W. Grand Lodge of South Carolina, have examined the "Masonic Trestle-Board," which has been just published by Brothers Moore and Carnegy, under the direction of the late National Masonic Convention, and we cheerfully recommend it to the patronage of the Fraternity. Masters of Lodges will find it of invaluable service while superintending the labors of the workmen, and to every Brother who seeks an increase of light it will afford important assistance. It is ornamented with the three "carpets," which are tastefully executed; that of the F. C. in particular is of an entirely original and very beautiful design. We therefore cordially unite with our Brethren of the Grand Lodge of Massachusetts in giving to it the sanction of our names.

GEO. B. ECKHARD, M. W. G. Master; JAMES C. NORRIS, Deputy Grand Master; JOHN B. IRVING, M. D., Senior Grand Warden; W. S. KING, Junior Grand Warden; ALBERT CASE, Grand Chaplain; JOHN H. HONOUR, Grand Treasurer; A. G. MACKEY, M. D. Grand Secretary; M. W. HENRY A. DESAUSSURE, P. G. Master; R. W. WM. B. FOSTER, P. D. G. Master.

At a communication of the M. W. Grand Lodge of New Hampshire, held at Portsmouth, Dec. 13, A. L. 5843, the following resolution was adopted, viz:

Resolved, By the M. W. Grand Lodge of New Hampshire, that the "MASONIC TRESTLE-BOARD" by R. W. Brothers Charles W. Moore and S. W. B. Carnegy, adapted to the National System of Work and Lectures as revised and perfected by the late U. S. Masonic Convention, be, and the same is hereby approved; and it is hereby ordered, that the same be used by the several Lodges under this jurisdiction, as a guide and text book in their labors. Attest, ISAAC L. FOLSOM, *G. Sec.*

The following Resolution was passed by the G. Lodge of Mass., Dec. 13, 1843.

Resolved, That the G. Lodge of Massachusetts recommend the "TRESTLE-BOARD" prepared by a Committee of the late National Convention, as a work embodying all the essentials of a Manual of Ancient Craft Masonry; and in preference to all other similar works, it especially sanctions to the subordinate Lodges under this jurisdiction, the use of this most excellent compend of the principles and ceremonials of the Order.

PREFACE.

This work has been prepared agreeably to a resolution of the National Masonic Convention, convened at Baltimore, (Md.,) in May, 1843.

The Convention was composed of Delegates from a majority of all the Grand Lodges in the United States. They were assembled for the purpose of revising and perfecting a uniform system of MASONIC WORK AND LECTURES. As an important auxiliary in the attainment of the great object of their appointment, they unanimously resolved "on the expediency of adopting a regularly authorized TRESTLE-BOARD," or Text-Book, for the use of the Lodges. And R. W. JOHN DOVE, Grand Secretary of the Grand Lodge of Virginia, R. W. CHARLES W. MOORE, Grand Secretary of the Grand Lodge of Massachusetts, and R. W. S. W. B. CARNEGY, Past Grand Master of the Grand Lodge of Missouri, were appointed to prepare the work. The result of the deliberations of a majority of the committee is herewith respectfully submitted to the Fraternity.

The Illustrations of the THREE DEGREES, and the ceremonies of the degree of Past Master, are given as they were collated and systematized, from Smith, Hutchinson, and their predecessors, by Preston, and adopted by Calcott, Webb, Dalcho, and other Masonic authors. The present editors have, however, endeavored to improve the style of their composition, and to adapt them to the condition and requirements of the Fraternity in the United States. The degree of success with which this has been accomplished, they leave to the decision of their Brethren.

A great amount of irrelevant and useless matter, with which our text-books are all more or less encumbered, has been rejected. Absurd and ridiculous pretensions are no more justifiable in societies than in individuals. Freemasonry requires only what fairly and honestly belongs to it. This will give it pre-eminence among all other Institutions of human origin. When its friends ask more than this, they ask more than sensible men are willing to concede.

It will be seen that the work is embellished with three fine engravings, representing the three CARPETS, illustrative of ancient Craft Masonry. The design of the second is new, as is also the arrangement of the emblems on the first and third. We cannot doubt that they will be equally acceptable and serviceable to our Brethren.

Such original matter has been introduced as was deemed essential to the general design of the work, and to the illustration of points in the ceremonies and history of the degrees, which might not otherwise be generally understood.

The utility of works of this description, will readily be conceded by every well informed Mason. The expediency of their publication is not now an open question. That was settled by our European Brethren more than a century ago. One of the Committee recently had in his hands a copy of a work of this class, published in England in the early part of the last century. The first publication of the kind in this country, was in the year 1734, by the illustrious Brother Dr. BENJAMIN FRANKLIN, then of Philadelphia. The illustrations in many of these early text-books, are as broad and copious as those contained in similar publications of more recent date.

A difference of opinion has prevented the work from appearing as the unanimous production of the committee. The respected Brother from Virginia, conceived that the retaining of many of the printed illustrations, which are contained in the Monitor and other similar works, was not desirable. To their omission the majority of the committee could not concede. They believed, that if these were left to be orally communicated, there would, in a few years, be as many different forms in use as there are Lodges; and that, consequently, *irregularity*, instead of *uniformity*, would be the result.

The great object of the publication is to facilitate the attainment, and to contribute to the preservation, of UNIFORMITY in the work of the Lodges. If it shall in any degree aid in accomplishing this, the important end proposed by the Convention in ordering its publication, will have been answered, and the fondest hopes of the committee realized.

CHARLES W. MOORE.
S. W. B. CARNEGY.

December, 1843.

CONTENTS.

	PAGE.
Apron, the	21
All-seeing eye,	43
Architecture, definition of,	32
Antiquity of,	32
Orders of,	32
Tuscan,	32
Doric,	32
Ionic,	33
Corinthian,	33
Composite,	33
Invention of,	33
Arithmetic,	36
Astronomy,	36
Address to Grand Master at his Installation,	78
at the initiation of a Clergyman,	79
at the initiation of a Foreigner,	79
at the initiation of a Soldier,	79
Anchor and Ark,	43
Badge of a Mason,	22
Brotherly Love,	25
Benediction,	14
Bee Hive,	42
Book of Constitutions,	42
Candidates, qualifications and duties of,	15
admisssion of,	18
Ceremonial illustrations,	19
Ceremony of constituting a Lodge,	47
of consecration,	52
Charges, at opening,	14
Charge at closing,	15
on the private duties of Masons,	16
on duties as Citizens,	17
on duties in the Lodge,	17
on duties as neighbors,	18
on duties towards a Brother,	18
at initiation to the first degree,	27
at initiation to the second degree,	38
at initiation to the third degree,	44
upon the installation of the officers of a Lodge,	68

	PAGE.
Ceremony of Installation,	54
laying of foundation stones,	61
Dedicating Masonic Halls,	64
to be observed at Funerals,	69
Closing a Lodge,	11
Common Gavel,	22
Corner Stones, laying of,	61
Declaration to be assented to by a Candidate,	19
Dedication of Masonic Halls,	64
of Lodges,	24
Emblems, the	42
Pot of Incense,	42
Bee Hive,	42
Book of Constitutions, &c.,	43
Sword pointing to a naked heart,	43
All-seeing Eye,	43
Anchor and Ark,	43
Fortyseventh Problem of Euclid,	43
Hour-Glass,	43
Scythe,	43
Three Steps,	44
Feeling,	34
First Degree,	20
first section of,	20
second section of,	22
third section of,	25
Five Senses,	34
Form of a Lodge,	23
Form of Petition for a new Lodge,	83
Dispensation for new Lodge,	83
Charter or Warrant,	84
Power for Constituting a new Lodge,	85
Commission for District Deputy Grand Master,	86
Commission reappointing the same,	87
Proxy for representation in Grand Lodge,	87
Fortitude,	25
Fortyseventh Problem of Euclid,	43
Freemasonry, definition of	9

CONTENTS.

	PAGE.
Funeral Ceremonies,	69
Do. Do.	73
Furniture of a Lodge,	23
Geometry,	36
advantages of,	36
moral advantages of,	37
Globes, use of	31
Grammar,	38
Hearing,	34
Hour-Glass,	43
Laying Foundation Stones,	61
Lamb Skin,	21
Lodge, definition of	9
its organization,	9
the form of,	23
the covering of,	23
the furniture of,	23
the ornaments of,	24
the jewels of,	24
to whom dedicated,	24
Logic,	35
Installation, ceremonies of	54
Jewels,	24
Justice,	26
Masonry, operative	29
speculative,	30
Music,	36
Opening of a Lodge,	10
Operative Masonry,	29
Past Master's Degree,	45
First section,	47
Second section,	54
Third section,	61
Fourth section,	64
Petition for Degrees,	18
Plumb line,	29
Prayer at opening on First Degree,	12
Second,	12
Third,	13
(general,)	13
do.	13
at closing on First Degree,	13
Second,	13

	PAGE.
Prayer, at closing on Third,	13
(general,)	14
(benediction,)	14
at the Initiation of a Candidate,	21
at Initiation to Second Degree,	29
to Third Degree,	41
at Funerals,	72
at Initiation,	80
Do.	80
Do.	81
at opening the Grand Lodge,	81
at Constituting a Lodge,	82
Procession, form of, at Constituting a Lodge,	49
of Grand Lodge at do.,	50
at laying foundation stones,	61
of Grand Lodge at do.,	61
at Dedications,	67
at Funerals,	70
Do.	74
Prudence,	25
Pot of Incense,	42
Remarks on the First Degree,	20
Second Degree,	28
Third Degree,	39
Past Master's Degree,	45
Relief,	25
Rhetoric,	35
Second Degree,	28
First Section,	28
Second Section,	29
Seven Liberal Arts and Sciences,	35
Seeing,	34
Smelling,	34
Six days, (illustrated,)	30
Speculative Masonry,	30
Scythe,	43
Tasting,	35
Temperance,	25
Third Degree, remarks on,	39
First Section,	40
Second Section,	40
Third Section,	41
Trowel, the	41
Truth,	25
Twentyfour inch Gauge,	22
Three Steps, the	44

ERRATUM.—In arranging the illustrations of the emblems on pages 42, 43, and 44, that of the THREE STEPS was accidentally placed *last*. It should have preceded the POT OF INCENSE, as in the plate.

THE TRESTLE-BOARD.

CHAPTER I.

FREEMASONRY — A LODGE — ITS ORGANIZATION.

"FREEMASONRY," says a learned foreign author, "is a MORAL ORDER, instituted by virtuous men, with the praiseworthy design of recalling to our remembrance the most sublime TRUTHS, in the midst of the most innocent and social pleasures,—founded on LIBERALITY, BROTHERLY-LOVE and CHARITY." It is a beautiful SYSTEM OF MORALITY, veiled in allegory and illustrated by symbols. TRUTH is its centre,—the external point whence its radii diverge, pointing out to its disciples a correct knowledge of the Great Architect of the Universe, and the moral laws which he has ordained for their government.

A LODGE OF MASONS consists of a certain number of Brethren, who are assembled together to expatiate on the mysteries of the Craft; having the HOLY BIBLE open on the Altar, to teach them the sacred principles of religion and justice,—the SQUARE and COMPASS, to remind them of the duties they owe to society and to themselves,—the BOOK OF CONSTITUTIONS, where they may study the general statutes of Masonry,—the BY-LAWS, to point out their duty as members of an individual Lodge,—and the WARRANT, or CHARTER, by virtue of which, having been issued by the Grand Lodge, they meet to transact the business of Masonry.

Any number of Masons, not less than seven, being well skilled in the work and mysteries of the Craft, and of good report among their Brethren, may petition the Grand Lodge, within the limits of whose jurisdiction they reside, for a Dispensation, authorizing them to ORGANIZE a Lodge for Masonic purposes. When organized, a Lodge consists of the Worshipful Master, Senior and Junior Wardens, Treasurer and Secretary, Senior and Junior Deacons, Senior and Junior Stewards, and as many members as a majority of the

Brethren may determine,—though more than fifty will generally be found inconvenient. In addition to the officers here enumerated, it is the indispensable duty of the Master of every Lodge, to appoint some trustworthy and skilful Brother to act as Tyler. A Marshal is also frequently appointed; but he is an officer of convenience, not of necessity.

CHAPTER II.

THE CEREMONIES OF OPENING AND CLOSING A LODGE.

The rites and ceremonies of Freemasonry form the distinctive peculiarity of the Institution. In their nature they are simple—in their end instructive. They naturally excite a high degree of curiosity in a newly initiated Brother, and create an earnest desire to investigate their meaning, and to become acquainted with their object and design. It requires, however, both serious application and untiring diligence, to ascertain the precise nature of every ceremony which our ancient Brethren saw reason to adopt in the formation of an exclusive system, which was to pass through the world, unconnected with the religion and politics of all times, and of every people among whom it should flourish and increase.* But the assiduous Mason, with the assistance of an intelligent Master in the Chair,—and none but intelligent Brethren should ever be placed in that responsible station,—will not fail to derive instruction from every ceremony he may witness, and improvement from every ordinance with which he may become acquainted.

The first business which occupies the Brethren, when assembled at their stated meetings, is what is technically termed the Opening of the Lodge. The ceremonies cannot here be described with any considerable degree of minuteness. We may however remark, that at the well known signal, the officers and members and visit-

---

*Philosophy of Freemasonry.

CEREMONIES OF OPENING AND CLOSING. 11

ing Brethren, clothed in their appropriate regalia, repair to their respective stations, and await the commands of the Worshipful Master. The avenues of the Lodge are secured, and the ceremony of opening proceeds.

The ceremony of closing differs from that of opening only in the necessary change of phraseology, and in certain precautionary measures. The Brethren present are all expected to assist in the performance of both duties, and much of the beauty and harmony of the scene depend on their quiet deportment and strict attention to the business before them. In this, as in all other Masonic ceremonies, everything like levity or rudeness in speech or action, is to be deprecated and avoided. A Mason should never forget that he is a gentleman, and that all the peculiarities he witnesses, or in which he is required to participate while in the Lodge, are designed to illustrate and inculcate some great moral truth. The peculiar beauty of our ceremonies is, that they all tend to improve the mind and consecrate the affections to virtue.

The labors and duties of the Lodge should begin and end with prayer. The Brethren cannot be too often reminded of their dependence on the Almighty Architect of the Universe for every blessing they enjoy. Prayer is an ancient and beautiful custom of the Institution. It was the constant practice of our ancestors. It is enjoined by the Constitutions, and cannot with propriety be dispensed with. There are also certain ancient Charges, one or more of which may be profitably rehearsed, either immediately subsequent to the opening, or just previously to the closing of the Lodge. And when business does not prevent, the reading of at least one of them, from the Book of Constitutions, ought never to be omitted. A knowledge of their duties to the Craft, to society, and to each other, cannot be too firmly fixed upon the minds of the Brethren.

It has been beautifully said, that the Master opens the Lodge at sunrise, with solemn prayer; the Junior Warden calls the men from labor when the Sun attains its meridian height; and the Senior Warden closes the Lodge with prayer at sunset,—when the labors of our ancient Brethren ended. The great luminary of creation rises in the East to open the day, with a mild and genial influence, and all nature rejoices in the appearance of his beams. He gains his meridian in the South, invigorating all things with the perfection of his ripening qualities. With declining strength he sets in the

West to close the day, leaving mankind at rest from their labors. This is a type of the three most pominent stages in the life of man—infancy, manhood, and age. The first, characterized by the blush of innocence, pure as the tints which gild the eastern portals of the day. The heart rejoices in the unsuspecting integrity of its own unblemished virtues, nor fears deceit, because it knows no guile. Manhood succeeds,—the ripening intellect arrives at the meridian of its powers, while at the approach of old age, his strength decays; his sun is setting in the West; and enfeebled by sickness or bodily infirmities, he lingers on till death finally closes his eventful day;—and happy is he, if the setting splendors of a virtuous life gild his departing moments with the gentle tints of hope; and close his short career in peace, harmony, and Brotherly-Love.

CHAPTER III.

PRAYERS AND CHARGES TO BE READ AT THE OPENING AND CLOSING OF LODGES.

PRAYERS.

PRAYER AT OPENING IN THE FIRST DEGREE.

The Worshipful Master says—Brethren: Before I declare the Lodge opened, let us invoke the assistance of the Great Architect of the Universe in all our undertakings. May our labors, thus begun in order, be conducted in peace, and closed in harmony.

Response.—So mote it be.

The Master then—In the name of God and Universal Benevolence, declares the Lodge duly opened for the purposes of Freemasonry in the first degree. * * *

AT OPENING IN THE SECOND DEGREE.

Master. Brethren—Before I declare the Lodge opened, let us fervently supplicate the Grand Geometrician of the Universe, that the rays of heaven may shed their benign influence over us, to enlighten us in the paths of virtue and science.

Response. So mote it be.

The Master then—In the name of the Grand Geometrician of the Universe, declares the Lodge duly opened on the Square, for the instruction and improvement of Craftsmen. * * *

PRAYERS AND CHARGES.

AT OPENING IN THE THIRD DEGREE.

Master. Brethren—Before I declare the Lodge opened, let us humbly supplicate the blessing of the Most High. May the labors of our present convocation be so conducted that the result thereof shall be acceptable to Him and honorable to our ancient Fraternity.

Response. So mote it be.

The Master then—In the name of the Most High, declares the Lodge duly opened on the centre, for the purposes of Freemasonry in the third degree. * * *

A GENERAL PRAYER AT OPENING.

Great Architect of the Universe—In thy name we have assembled, and in thy name we desire to proceed in all our doings. Grant that the sublime principles of Freemasonry, may so subdue every discordant passion within us—so harmonize and enrich our hearts with thine own love and goodness—that the Lodge at this time, may humbly reflect that order and beauty which reign forever before thy throne. Amen.

Response. So mote it be.

ANOTHER.

Supreme Architect of the Universe—We invoke thy blessing at this time: May this meeting thus begun in order, be conducted in peace, and closed in harmony. Amen.

Response. So mote it be.

AT CLOSING IN THE FIRST DEGREE.

Master. Brethren—Before I declare the Lodge closed, let us, with all reverence and humility, express our gratitude to the Great Architect of the Universe, for the favors already received. May he continue to preserve the Order, by cementing and adorning it with every social and moral virtue.

Response. So mote it be.

AT CLOSING IN THE SECOND DEGREE.

Master. Brethren—Before I declare the Lodge closed, let us humbly invoke the continued blessing of the Grand Geometrician of the Universe, on our Fraternity. Let us remember that wherever we are, and whatever we do, He is with us—that His All-Seeing Eye observes us. While, then, we continue to act in conformity with the principles of the Craft, let us not fail to discharge our duties towards Him, with fervency and zeal.

Response. So mote it be.

AT CLOSING IN THE THIRD DEGREE.

Master. Brethren—Before I declare the Lodge closed, let us unite in humbly acknowledging our dependence on the Most High. May his right hand be as a shield and buckler to us against the assaults of our enemies; and at the final day, may each and every one of us, be raised, through the merits of the Lion of the tribe of Judah, to the celestial Lodge above, where the Supreme Grand Master forever presides—forever reigns.

Response. So mote it be.

A GENERAL PRAYER AT CLOSING.

Supreme Grand Master! Ruler of Heaven and Earth! Now that we are about to separate and to return to our respective places of abode, wilt thou be pleased so to influence our hearts and minds, that we may each one of us, practice out of the Lodge, those great moral duties which are inculcated in it, and with reverence study and obey the laws which thou hast given us in thy Holy Word. Amen.

Response. So mote it be.

BENEDICTON.

May the blessing of Heaven rest upon us, and all regular Masons! May Brotherly-Love prevail, and every moral and social virtue cement us! Amen.

Response. So mote it be.

CHARGES.

CHARGE AT OPENING.

The ways of Virtue are beautiful. Knowledge is attained by degrees. Wisdom dwells with contemplation. There we must seek her. Let us, then, Brethren, apply ourselves with becoming zeal to the practice of the excellent principles inculcated by our Order. Let us ever remember that the great objects of our association, are the restraint of improper desires and passions, the cultivation of an active benevolence, and the promotion of a correct knowledge of the duties we owe to God, our neighbor, and ourselves. Let us be united, and practice with assiduity the sacred tenets of our Order. Let all private animosities, if any unhappily exist, give place to affection and Brotherly-Love. It is a useless parade to talk of the subjection of irregular passions within the walls of the Lodge, if we permit them to triumph in our intercourse with each other. Uniting in the grand design, let us be happy ourselves, and endeavor to promote the happiness of others. Let us cultivate the great moral virtues which are laid down on our Masonic Trestle-Board, and improve in every thing that is good, amiable and useful. Let the benign Genius of the Mystic Art preside over our councils, and under her sway let us act with a dignity becoming the high moral character of our venerable Institution.

ANOTHER CHARGE AT OPENING.

"Behold, how good and how pleasant it is for Brethren to dwell together in unity!

"It is like the precious ointment upon the head, that ran down upon the beard, even Aaron's beard, that went down to the skirts of his garment:

"As the dew of Hermon, and as the dew that descended upon the mountains of Zion: for there the Lord commanded the blessing, even life forevermore."

CHARGE AT CLOSING.

Brethren: You are now to quit this sacred retreat of friendship and virtue, to mix again with the world. Amidst its concerns and employments, forget not the duties you have heard so frequently inculcated and forcibly recommended in this Lodge. Be diligent, prudent, temperate, discreet. Remember, that around this altar you have promised to befriend and relieve every Brother, who shall need your assistance. Remember, that you have promised to remind him, in the most tender manner, of his failings, and aid his reformation. Vindicate his character, when wrongfully traduced. Suggest in his behalf the most candid and favorable circumstances. Is he justly reprehended?—let the world observe how Masons love one another.

These generous principles are to extend farther. Every human being has a claim upon your kind offices. "Do good unto all." Recommend it more "especially to the household of the FAITHFUL."

By diligence in the duties of your respective callings; by liberal benevolence and diffusive charity; by constancy and fidelity in your friendships, discover the beneficial and happy effects of this ancient and honorable Institution.

Let it not be supposed that you have here "LABORED in vain, and spent your STRENGTH for nought; for your WORK is with the LORD, and your RECOMPENSE with your GOD."

Finally, Brethren, be ye all of one mind,—live in peace, and may the God of love and peace delight to dwell with and bless you!

CHAPTER IV.

ON THE QUALIFICATIONS AND DUTIES OF CANDIDATES FOR FREEMASONRY.

"WHOSOEVER, from love of knowledge, interest or curiosity," say the Constitutions, "desires to be a FREEMASON, is to know, that, as his foundation and great corner-stone, he is to believe firmly in the ETERNAL GOD, and to pay that worship which is due to him as the Great Architect and Governor of the Universe. A Freemason is obliged by his tenure to observe the moral law; and if he rightly understand the art, he cannot tread in the irreligious paths of the unhappy LIBERTINE, or stupid ATHEIST; nor, in any case, act against the great inward light of his own conscience.

"He will likewise shun the gross errors of bigotry and superstition; making a due use of his own reason, according to that liberty, wherewith a Mason is made free. He is charged to adhere to those grand essentials of religion, in which all men agree; leaving each Brother to his own private judgment, as to particular modes and forms. Whence it follows, that all Freemasons are to be GOOD MEN AND TRUE,—men of honor and honesty,—by whatever religious names or persuasions distinguished,—always following the golden precept, " of doing unto all men as they would that all men should do unto them," and of worshipping God after that manner and form which they conscientiously believe to be most acceptable in his sight."

Another of the Constitutions, further provides, that no person shall be admitted a member, unless he be " free born; of mature and discreet age;* of good report; of sufficient natural endowments, and the senses of a man; with an estate, office, trade, occupation, or some visible way of acquiring an honest livelihood, and of working in his craft, as becomes the members of this most Ancient and Honorable Fraternity, who ought not only to earn what is sufficient for themselves and families, but likewise something to spare for works of CHARITY, and supporting the true dignity of the Craft."

* * * * * * *

" No Brother shall propose for admission into this ancient and honorable Society, any person, through friendship or partiality, who does not possess the moral and social virtues, a sound head and a good heart; and who has not an entire exemption from all those ill qualities and vices, which would bring dishonor on the Craft."

ANCIENT CHARGES.

THE PRIVATE DUTIES OF MASONS.

WHOEVER would be a Mason should know how to practice all the private virtues. He should avoid all manner of intemperance or excess, which might prevent his performance of the laudable duties of his craft, or lead him into enormities, which would reflect dishonor upon the ancient Fraternity. He is to be industrious in his profession, and true to the Master he serves. He is to labor justly, and not to eat any man's bread for nought; but to pay truly for his meat and drink. What leisure his labor allows, he is to employ in studying the arts and sciences with a diligent mind, that he may the better perform all his duties, to his Creator, his country, his neighbor, and himself.

---

*Not under twentyone years.

He is to seek and acquire, as far as possible, the virtues of patience, meekness, self-denial, forbearance, and the like, which give him the command over himself, and enable him to govern his own family with affection, dignity and prudence: at the same time checking every disposition injurious to the world, and promoting that love and service which Brethren of the same household owe to each other.

Therefore, to afford succour to the distressed, to divide our bread with the industrious poor, and to put the misguided traveller into the way, are duties of the Craft, suitable to its dignity, and expressive of its usefulness. But, though a Mason is never to shut his ear unkindly against the complaints of any of the human race, yet when a Brother is oppressed or suffers, he is in a more peculiar manner called to open his whole soul in love and compassion to him, and to relieve him without prejudice, according to his capacity.

It is also necessary, that all who would be true Masons should learn to abstain from all malice, slander and evil speaking; from all provoking, reproachful and ungodly language: keeping always a tongue of good report.

A Mason should know how to obey those who are set over him; however inferior they may be in worldly rank or condition. For although Masonry divests no man of his honors and titles, yet, in the Lodge, pre-eminence of virtue, and knowledge in the art, is considered as the true source of all nobility, rule and government.

The virtue indispensably requisite in Masons is—SECRECY. This is the guard of their confidence, and the security of their trust. So great stress is to be laid upon it, that it is enforced under the strongest obligations; nor, in their esteem, is any man to be accounted wise, who has not intellectual strength and ability sufficient to cover and conceal such honest secrets as are committed to him, as well as his own more serious and private affairs.

DUTIES AS CITIZENS.

A MASON is a peaceable citizen, and is never to be concerned in plots and conspiracies against the peace and welfare of the nation, nor to behave himself undutifully to inferior magistrates. He is cheerfully to conform to every lawful authority; to uphold, on every occasion, the interest of the community, and zealously promote the prosperity of his own country. Masonry has ever flourished in times of peace, and been always injured by war, bloodshed, and confusion; so that kings and princes, in every age, have been much disposed to encourage the craftsmen on account of their peaceableness and loyalty, whereby they practically answer the cavils of their adversaries and promote the honor of the Fraternity. Craftsmen are bound by peculiar ties to promote peace, cultivate harmony, and live in concord and Brotherly Love.

DUTIES IN THE LODGE.

WHILE the Lodge is open for work, Masons must hold no private conversation or committees, without leave from the Master; nor talk of anything foreign or impertinent; nor interrupt the Master or Wardens, or any Brother addressing himself to the Chair; nor behave inattentively, while the Lodge is engaged in what is serious and solemn; but every Brother shall pay due reverence to the Master, the Wardens, and all his fellows.

Every Brother guilty of a fault shall submit to the Lodge, unless he appeal to the Grand Lodge.

No private offences, or disputes about nations, families, religions, or politics, must be brought within the doors of the Lodge.

DUTIES AS NEIGHBORS.

Masons ought to be moral men. Consequently they should be good husbands, good parents, good sons, and good neighbors; avoiding all excess, injurious to themselves or families, and wise as to all affairs, both of their own household and of the Lodge, for certain reasons known to themselves.

DUTIES TOWARDS A BROTHER.

Free and Accepted Masons have ever been charged to avoid all slander of true and faithful Brethren, and all malice and unjust resentment, or talking disrespectfully of a Brother's person or performance. Nor must they suffer any to spread unjust reproaches or calumnies against a Brother behind his back, nor to injure him in his fortune, occupation or character; but they shall defend such a Brother, and give him notice of any danger or injury wherewith he may be threatened, to enable him to escape the same, as far as is consistent with honor, prudence, and the safety of religion, morality, and the state; but no farther.

CHAPTER V.

ADMISSION OF CANDIDATES.

By the regulations of the Fraternity, no candidate for the mysteries of Masonry can be initiated in any regular Lodge, without having stood proposed one lunar month, unless a dispensation be obtained in his favor. All applications for initiation should be made in writing, and in the following form:

" *To the Worshipful Master, Wardens and Brethren, of
———— Lodge, of Ancient Free and Accepted Masons.*

"The petition of the subscriber respectfully represents, that having long entertained a favorable opinion of your ancient Institution, he is desirous, if found worthy, of being admitted a member thereof.

"His place of residence is ———, his age —— years, his occupation ———.

  (Signed,)   A. B."

[Recommended by three or more members of the Lodge.]

This petition, having been read in open Lodge, is placed on file. A committee is then appointed to investigate the character and qualifications of the petitioner. If, at the next regular meeting of the

Lodge, the report of the committee be favorable, and the candidate is admitted, he is taken to an adjoining apartment, and required to give his free and full assent to the following interrogations :

1. "Do you seriously declare, upon your honor, before these gentlemen,[*] that, unbiased by friends, and uninfluenced by mercenary motives, you freely and voluntarily offer yourself a candidate for the mysteries of Masonry ?"

2. "Do you seriously declare, upon your honor, before these gentlemen, that you are prompted to solicit the privileges of Masonry by a favorable opinion conceived of the Institution, a desire of knowledge, and a sincere wish of being serviceable to your fellow creatures ?"

3. "Do you seriously declare, upon your honor, before these gentlemen, that you will cheerfully conform to all the ancient established usages and customs of the Fraternity ?"

The candidate, if no objections be urged to the contrary, is then introduced in due and ancient form.

CHAPTER VI.

CEREMONIAL ILLUSTRATIONS.

GENERAL REMARKS.

ANCIENT CRAFT MASONRY is divided into three degrees. It was probably so divided at the building of King Solomon's Temple, with the design to bear a general reference to the three Orders of the Jewish Priesthood. The same arrangement was subsequently adopted by the Christian church. It also prevailed in all the ancient mysteries. In a majority of them the first step, or degree, consisted of probation, purification, and expiation. The second was called the Lesser Mysteries,—into which the candidate passed by solemn ceremonies. The third,—to which he was advanced after a long period of additional trial,—was denominated the Greater Mysteries.

---

[*]The Stewards of the Lodge are usually present.

These consisted of fearful rites, introductory to a full revelation of all the ineffable doctrines taught by the Priests ; and which the candidate was bound, under an obligation and heavy penalties, never to reveal.

The Essenes, who, says Dr. Oliver, preserved the true Freemasonry from extinction in the dark ages which preceded the advent of Christ, admitted only three steps, or degrees, and the probationary term extended to one year. If, during this period, the candidate gave satisfactory proofs of his temperance, fortitude, prudence, and justice, he was accepted, and received the first degree. In this noviciate he remained another year, before he was passed to the second degree ; and it was not until the expiration of three years, that he was admitted to a full participation in the secrets and benefits of the society. And even then the utmost precaution was used. The candidate was previously bound by the most solemn vows, to keep inviolably secret the mysteries of his Order ; and to act upon and abide by the ancient usages and established customs of the Fraternity. The Brethren distinguished each other in darkness and in light, by peculiar signals. The most profound silence was imposed at their assemblies ; the Lecturer only, expounding the tenets of their creed,—which were enfolded in a series of allegorical symbols,—the rest listening with a grave and solemn attention.

REMARKS ON THE FIRST DEGREE.

FIRST SECTION.

It has been truly remarked, that the first step taken by a candidate on entering a Lodge of Freemasons, teaches him the pernicious tendency of infidelity, and shows him that the foundation on which Masonry rests, is the belief and acknowledgment of a Supreme Being; that in Him alone a sure confidence can be safely placed, to protect his steps in all the dangers and difficulties he may be called on to encounter in his progress through life ; and it assures him, that, if his faith be well founded in that Being, he may confidently pursue his course without fear and without danger. The first section of the degree also teaches him, that he is to take the Holy Bible as the rule and guide of his faith,—that he is to square his actions by the precepts therein contained,—to circumscribe his desires and passions within the compass of virtue and morality,—and to relieve the necessities of others, with the superfluities of his own substance.

A full and perfect knowledge of this section is indispensably necessary to every Mason, who would be serviceable to the Institution, or avail himself of its privileges and its enjoyments. It is the alphabet of Masonry, and must be learned before any progress can be made in the more abstruse and important branches of the study. It consists in general heads, which, while they serve as marks of distinction, enable us not only to try and examine the rights of others, but to prove ourselves.

PRAYER USED AT THE INITIATION OF A CANDIDATE.

Vouchsafe thine aid, Almighty Father of the Universe, to this our present convention; and grant that this candidate for Masonry, may dedicate and devote his life to thy service, and become a true and faithful Brother among us. Endue him with a competency of thy divine Wisdom, that by the influence of the pure principles of our Order, he may the better be enabled to display the beauties of holiness, to the honor of thy holy name. Amen.

Response. So mote it be.

It is the duty of the Master of the Lodge, as one of the precautionary measures of initiation, to explain to the candidate the nature and design of the Institution. And while he informs him, that it is founded on the purest principles of piety and virtue, that it possesses great and invaluable privileges, and that in order to secure those privileges to worthy men, and worthy men alone, voluntary pledges of fidelity are required,—he will at the same time assure him, that nothing will be expected of him, incompatible with his civil, moral or religious duties.

In the course of this section, is given an explanation of that peculiar and appropriate ensign of Freemasonry,

THE LAMB SKIN, OR WHITE LEATHER APRON.

It is an emblem of innocence, and the badge of a Mason,—more ancient than the Golden Fleece, or Roman Eagle,—more honorable than the Star and Garter, or any other Order, that can be conferred upon the candidate at the time of his initiation, or at any future period, by king, prince, potentate, or any other person, except he be a Mason; and which it is presumed he will wear with equal pleasure to himself and honor to the Fraternity.

This section closes with a moral explication of the TWENTY-FOUR INCH GAUGE and COMMON GAVEL.

THE TWENTYFOUR INCH GAUGE

Is an instrument made use of by operative Masons, to measure and lay out their work. But we, as free and accepted Masons, are taught to make use of it for the more noble and glorious purpose of dividing our time. It being divided into twentyfour parts, is emblematical of the twenty-four hours of the day; which we are taught to divide into three parts, whereby we find a portion for the service of God and a distressed worthy Brother; a portion for our usual avocations; and a portion for refreshment and sleep.

THE COMMON GAVEL

Is an instrument made use of by operative Masons, to break off the rough and superfluous parts of stones, the better to fit them for the builder's use; but we, as free and accepted Masons, are taught to make use of it for the more noble and glorious purpose of divesting our minds and consciencies of all the vices and superfluities of life, thereby fitting ourselves as living stones, for that spiritual building, that house not made with hands, eternal in the heavens.

SECOND SECTION.

THIS section is altogether explanatory of the preceding one. It beautifully and comprehensively illustrates the ceremonies of initiation; and while it gratifies, it cannot fail to impress the mind of the intelligent and right-hearted candidate, with a high sense of the great moral excellencies of the degree through which he is passing. It does not, however, admit of printed illustrations. We may only add, that the Lamb Skin, or white Leather Apron, is

THE BADGE OF A MASON.

The Lamb has in all ages been deemed an emblem of innocence. He, therefore, who wears the Lamb Skin as the "Badge of a Mason," is continually reminded of that purity of life and conduct, which is essentially necessary to his gaining admission into the Celestial Lodge above, where the Supreme Architect of the Universe presides.

THIRD SECTION.

THE third and last section of this degree is, perhaps, the most interesting and instructive of the three. Nor is a perfect knowledge of it less essential to a proper understanding of the ceremonies of initiation. Indeed, the Brother who has not made himself familiar with it, need not be at the trouble of urging his claims to any great proficiency as a Mason. The principal points illustrated by it are— 1. The FORM.—2. The SUPPORTS.—3. The COVERING.—4. The FURNITURE.—5. The ORNAMENTS.—6. The LIGHTS.—7. The JEWELS.—8. The SITUATION—and 9. The DEDICATION, of Lodges.

Lodge meetings, at the present day, are usually held in upper chambers,—probably for the better security which such places afford. It may be, however, that the custom had its origin in a practice observed by the ancient Jews, of building their temples, schools, and synagogues, on high hills,—a practice which seems to have met with the approbation of the Almighty, who said unto the prophet Ezekiel, "upon the top of the mountain, the whole limit thereof, round about, shall be most holy." Before the erection of temples, the *celestial* bodies were worshipped on HILLS, and the *terrestial* ones in VALLEYS. At a later period, the Christians, wherever it was practicable, erected their churches on eminences. And it is worthy of remark, that, according to Masonic traditionary history, the oldest Lodge in England was, at one time, held in a crypt beneath the foundations of York Cathedral. But it matters not whence the custom originated. It is a very safe and proper one. The FORM of a Lodge is familiar to every Mason.

A Lodge is metaphorically said to be SUPPORTED by three great pillars, called Wisdom, Strength, and Beauty ; because it is necessary that there should be Wisdom to contrive, Strength to support, and Beauty to adorn, all great and important undertakings.

And the COVERING is no less than the cloudy canopy of heaven, whither all good Masons hope at last to arrive, by aid of the theological ladder which Jacob in his vision saw reaching from earth to heaven,—the three principal rounds of which are denominated Faith, Hope, and Charity,—teaching faith in God, hope in immortality, and charity to all mankind.

Every well governed Lodge is FURNISHED with the Holy Bible, Square, and Compass.

> The Bible is dedicated to the service of God, it being the inestimable gift of God to man; * * * the Square to the Master, it being the proper Masonic emblem of his office, and the Compass to the Craft, because, by a due attention to its use, they are taught to regulate their desires, and to keep their passions within due bounds with all mankind, but more especially with their Brethren in Freemasonry.

The ORNAMENTS of a Lodge are the Mosaic Pavement, the Indented Tessel, and the Blazing Star.

The MOSAIC PAVEMENT is a representation of the ground floor of King Solomon's Temple; the INDENTED TESSEL, of that beautiful tesselated border, or skirting, which surrounded it,—the BLAZING STAR was in the centre. The MOSAIC PAVEMENT is emblematical of human life, chequered with good and evil; the INDENTED TESSEL which surrounds it, of those manifold blessings and comforts which surround us, and which we hope to obtain by a faithful reliance on Divine Providence, which is hieroglyphically represented by the BLAZING STAR in the centre.

The MOVABLE and IMMOVABLE JEWELS, are also explained in this section. The latter according to the present system, are worn by the first three officers of the Lodge. The former, properly belong on or near the three pedestals.

The ROUGH ASHLER is a stone as taken from the quarry, in its rude and natural state. The PERFECT ASHLER is a stone made ready by the hands of the Apprentice to be adjusted by the working tools of the Fellow Craft. The TRESTLE-BOARD is for the Master to draw his designs upon.

By the ROUGH ASHLER we are reminded of our rude and imperfect state by nature; by the PERFECT ASHLER, of that state of perfection at which we hope to arrive, by a virtuous education, our own endeavors, and the blessing of God; and by the TRESTLE-BOARD, we are also reminded, that as the operative workman erects his temporal building agreeably to the rules and designs laid down by the Master on his Trestle-Board, so should we, as speculative Masons, endeavor to erect our spiritual building agreeably to the rules and designs laid down by the Supreme Architect of the Universe, in the great volume of nature and revelations, which is our moral and Masonic Trestle-Board.

Lodges in ancient times were DEDICATED to King Solomon. We have a tradition which informs us, that they were thus dedicated from the building of the first Temple at Jerusalem to the Babylonish captivity; from thence to the coming of the Messiah, they were dedicated to Zerubbabel, the builder of the second Temple; and from that time to the final destruction of the Temple by Titus, in the reign of the Emperor Vespasian, they were dedicated to St. John the Baptist. The tradition goes on to say, that owing to the many massacres and disorders which attended that memorable event, Freemasonry fell very much into decay. Many of the Lodges were entirely broken up, and but few could meet in sufficient numbers to constitute their legality. Under these circumstances, a general meeting of the Craft was held in the city of Benjamin, when it was observed, that the principal reason for the decline of Masonry, was the want of a Grand Master to direct its affairs. They therefore deputed seven of their most eminent members to wait upon St. John the Evangelist, who was at that time Bishop of Ephesus, to request him to take the office of Grand Master. He returned for answer, that though well stricken in years, (being upwards of ninety,) yet having been in the early part of his life initiated into Masonry, he would take upon himself that office. He did so, and thereby completed by his learning, what the other St. John had accomplished by his zeal, and thus drew what the old records term a line-parallel. After his decease the Christian Lodges were dedicated to him and St. John the Baptist, they both being regarded as eminent Christian patrons of Freemasonry.

Since their time, there has been represented in every regular and well-furnished Lodge, a certain POINT WITHIN A CIRCLE, embordered by two perpendicular parallel lines, representing St. John the Baptist and St. John the Evangelist. Upon the vertex of the Circle rests the Book of Masonic Constitutions,—the Point represents an individual Brother,—the Circle, the boundary line of his duty. In going round this Circle, we necessarily touch on the two parallel lines, as well as on the Book of Constitutions; and while a Mason keeps himself circumscribed within their precepts, it is impossible that he should materially err.

The Principal Point of Masonry is three fold, and comprises the exalted virtues of Brotherly Love, Relief, and Truth—which are the tenets of a Mason's profession. They are thus explained:

BROTHERLY LOVE.

By the exercise of Brotherly Love, we are taught to regard the whole human species as one family,—the high and low, the rich and poor; who, as created by one Almighty Parent, and inhabitants of the same planet, are to aid, support and protect each other. On this principle, Masonry unites men of every country, sect and opinion, and conciliates true friendship among those who might otherwise have remained at a perpetual distance.

RELIEF.

To relieve the distressed is a duty incumbent on all men; but particularly on Masons, who are linked together by an indissoluble chain of sincere affection. To soothe the unhappy, to sympathize with their misfortunes, to compassionate their miseries, and to restore peace to their troubled minds, is the grand aim we have in view. On this basis we form our friendships, and establish our connexions.

TRUTH.

Truth is a divine attribute, and the foundation of every virtue. To be good and true, is the first lesson we are taught in Masonry. On this theme we contemplate, and by its dictates endeavor to regulate our conduct. Hence, while influenced by this principle, hypocrisy and deceit are unknown among us, sincerity and plain dealing distinguish us, and the heart and tongue join in promoting each other's welfare, and rejoicing in each other's prosperity.

To this explanation of the above principles, succeeds an illustration of the four cardinal virtues,—Temperance, Fortitude, Prudence and Justice :

TEMPERANCE

Is that due restraint upon our affections and passions, which renders the body tame and governable, and frees the mind from the allurements of vice. This virtue should be the constant practice of every Mason, as he is thereby taught to avoid excess or the contracting of any licentious or vicious habit, the indulgence in which might lead him to disclose some of those valuable secrets, which he has promised to conceal and never reveal, and which would consequently subject him to the contempt and detestation of all good Masons. * * *

FORTITUDE

Is that noble and steady purpose of the mind, whereby we are enabled to undergo any pain, peril or danger, when prudentially deemed expedient. This virtue is equally distant from rashness and cowardice ; and, like the former, should be deeply impressed upon the mind of every Mason, as a safeguard or security against any illegal attack that may be made, by force or otherwise, to extort from him any of those valuable secrets with which he has been so solemnly entrusted, and which was emblematically represented upon his first admission into the Lodge. * * *

PRUDENCE

Teaches us to regulate our lives and actions agreeably to the dictates of reason, and is that habit by which we wisely judge, and prudentially determine, on all things relative to our present as well as to our future happiness. This virtue should be the peculiar characteristic of every Mason, not only for the government of his conduct while in the Lodge, but also when abroad in the world. It should be particularly attended to in all strange and mixed companies, that the secrets of Masonry may not be unlawfully obtained. * * *

JUSTICE

Is that standard, or boundary of right, which enables us to render to every man his just due. This virtue is not only consistent with divine and human laws, but is the very cement and support of civil society ; and, as Justice in a great measure constitutes the real good man, so should it be the invariable practice of every Mason never to deviate from the minutest principles thereof. * * *

The illustration of these virtues is accompanied with some general observations peculiar to Masons.

Such is the arrangement of the different sections in the first lecture, which, with the forms adopted at the opening and closing of a Lodge, comprehends the whole of the first degree of Masonry. This plan has the advantage of regularity to recommend it, the support of precedent and authority, and the sanction and respect which flow from antiquity.

CHARGE AT INITIATION INTO THE FIRST DEGREE.

My Brother:—Having passed through the ceremonies of your initiation, allow me to congratulate you on your admission into our ancient and honorable Fraternity. Ancient, as having existed from time immemorial; honorable, as tending to make all men so who are strictly obedient to its precepts. It is an Institution having for its foundation the practice of the social and moral virtues. And to so high an eminence has its credit been advanced, that in every age and country, men pre-eminent for their moral and intellectual attainments, have encouraged and promoted its interests. Nor has it been thought derogatory to their dignity that monarchs have for a season exchanged the sceptre for the trowel, to patronize our mysteries, and join in our assemblies.

As a Mason, you are to regard the volume of the Sacred Law, as the great light in your profession; to consider it as the unerring standard of truth and justice, and to regulate your actions by the divine precepts it contains. In it you will learn the important duties you owe to God, your neighbor, and yourself. *To God*, by never mentioning his name, but with that awe and reverence which are due from the creature to his Creator; by imploring his aid on all your lawful undertakings, and by looking up to him in every emergency, for comfort and support. *To your neighbor*, by acting with him upon the square; by rendering him every kind office which justice or mercy may require; by relieving his distresses, and soothing his afflictions; and by doing to him, as in similar cases, you would that he should do unto you. And *to yourself*, by such a prudent and well regulated course of discipline, as may best conduce to the preservation of your corporeal and mental faculties in their fullest energy; thereby enabling you to exert the talents wherewith God has blest you, as well to his glory, as to the welfare of your fellow creatures.

As a Citizen, you are enjoined to be exemplary in the discharge of your civil duties, by never proposing, or countenancing, any act which may have a tendency to subvert the peace and good order of society; by paying due obedience to the laws under whose protection you live, and by never losing sight of the allegiance due to your country.

As an individual, you are charged to practice the domestic and public virtues. Let *Temperance* chasten, *Fortitude* support, *Prudence* direct you, and *Justice* be the guide of all your actions. Be especially careful to maintain, in their fullest splendor, those truly Masonic ornaments, which have already been amply illustrated,—*Brotherly Love, Relief* and *Truth*.

Finally: Be faithful to the trust committed to your care, and manifest your fidelity to your principles, by a strict observance of the constitutions of the Fraternity; by adhering to the ancient land-marks of the Order; and by refraining to recommend any one to a participation in our privileges, unless you have strong grounds to believe that, by a similar fidelity, he will ultimately reflect honor on our ancient Institution.

CHAPTER VII.

REMARKS ON THE SECOND DEGREE.

LIKE all sciences, whether moral or physical, Freemasonry is progressive, and a perfect knowledge of it can only be acquired by time, patience, and a sedulous application to elementary principles. The first degree is admirably calculated to enforce the duties of morality, and imprint on the memory some of the noblest principles which can enrich and adorn the mind. The second degree extends the same plan, but comprehends a more diffusive system of moral science. A more enlarged view is presented to the mind of the candidate. The heart is improved, while the ideas expand under a course of training which blends interest with instruction. And all the illustrations tend to inculcate a knowledge of those three great branches of Masonic morality and true religion—the duties we owe to God, our neighbor, and ourselves.

FIRST SECTION.

The first section of this degree is initiatory, and should be familiar to every Craftsman, but particularly to the officers of the Lodge. If properly illustrated, the candidate is deeply impressed with the importance of the ceremonies through which he is passing, and of the necessity of adhering to all the established usages of the Order.

PRAYER TO BE USED IN THIS DEGREE.

We supplicate the continuance of thine aid, O Merciful Lord, in behalf of ourselves, and the candidate who kneels before thee. May the work begun in thy name, be continued to thy glory, and evermore be established in us, in obedience to thy divine precepts. Amen.

Response. So mote it be.

The following passage of Scripture is generally read by the Master:

"Though I speak with the tongues of men and of angels, and have not charity, I am become as sounding brass, or a tinkling cymbal. And though I have the gift of prophecy, and understand all mysteries, and all knowledge; and though I have all faith, so that I could remove mountains, and have not charity, I am nothing. And though I bestow all my goods to

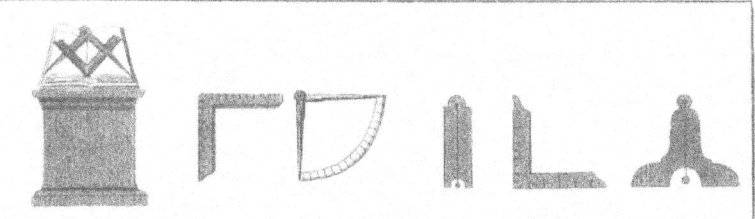

feed the poor, and though I give my body to be burned, and have not charity, it profiteth me nothing. Charity suffereth long, and is kind; charity envieth not; charity vaunteth not itself, is not puffed up, doth not behave itself unseemly, seeketh not her own, is not easily provoked, thinketh no evil; rejoiceth not in iniquity, but rejoiceth in the truth; beareth all things, believeth all things, hopeth all things, endureth all things. * * *
And now abideth faith, hope, charity, these three; but the greatest of these is charity." 1 Cor. ch. xiii.

The PLUMB, SQUARE and LEVEL, are implements peculiar to this degree.

The PLUMB is an instrument made use of by operative Masons, to try perpendiculars; the SQUARE, to square their work; and the LEVEL, to prove horizontals; but we, as Free and Accepted Masons, are taught to make use of them for more noble and glorious purposes. The Plumb admonishes us to walk uprightly in our several stations before God and man, squaring our actions by the square of virtue, ever remembering that we are travelling upon the level of time, to "that undiscovered country, from whose bourne no traveller returns."

SECOND SECTION.

The second section of this degree is principally devoted to the explication of physical science, and the tracing of the goodness and majesty of the Creator, by minutely analyzing his works. The intellectual faculties expand as a desire of knowledge increases. By the studies attached to this section, the mind is elevated to a communion with its Maker. What a sublime field for moral investigation and critical research do the seven liberal arts and sciences afford! The subtleties of Grammar, Rhetoric and Logic—the wonderful combinations of Arithmetic—the universal application of Geometry—the delicacy of Music, and the sublimity of Astronomy, have each a separate charm to win the heart and point to a Creator. Circumstances of importance to the Craft, and of peculiar interest to the Mason who delights in the study of the mystic beauties of his profession, are here developed and explained. We may however, only add, that Masonry is considered under two denominations —operative and speculative.

OPERATIVE MASONRY.

By operative Masonry, we allude to a proper application of the useful rules of architecture, whence a structure will derive figure, strength, and beauty, and whence will result a due proportion and just correspondence in all its parts. It furnishes us with dwellings, and convenient shelters from the vicissitudes and inclemencies of the seasons; and while it displays the effects of human wisdom, as well in the choice as in the arrangement of the sundry materials of which an edifice is composed, it demonstrates that a fund of science and industry is implanted in man, for the best, most salutary, and beneficent purposes.

SPECULATIVE MASONRY.

By speculative Masonry we learn to subdue the passions, act upon the square, keep a tongue of good report, maintain secrecy, and practise charity. It is so far interwoven with religion, as to lay us under obligations to pay that rational homage to the Deity, which at once constitutes our duty and our happiness. It leads the contemplative to view with reverence and admiration the glorious works of the creation, and inspires him with the most exalted ideas of the perfections of his divine Creator.

IN SIX DAYS

God created the heavens and the earth, and rested upon the seventh day; the seventh, therefore, our ancient Brethren consecrated as a day of rest from their labors, thereby enjoying frequent opportunities to contemplate the glorious works of the creation, and to adore their great Creator.*

---

* THE SIX DAYS, may be more particularly illustrated as follows:

Before the Almighty was pleased to command this vast world into existence, the elements and materials of creation lay blended together without distinction or form. Darkness was on the face of the great deep, and the spirit of God moved on the surface of the waters. The Almighty, as an example to man, that all things of moment should be done with due deliberation, was pleased to be SIX DAYS in commanding it from chaos to perfection. The FIRST instance of his supreme power was made manifest by commanding light; and being pleased with this new operation, he distinguished it by name, calling the light day, and the darkness he called night. And in order to keep this same framed matter within just limits, the SECOND DAY was employed in laying the foundation for the heavens, which he called firmament, designed to keep the waters that were within the clouds and those beneath them, asunder. On the THIRD DAY, he commanded those waters within due limits, and dry land appeared, which he called earth; and the mighty congregated waters he called sea. The earth being yet irregular and barren, God spoke the word and it was immediately covered with a beautiful carpet of grass, designed as pasture for the brute creation. Trees, shrubs and flowers of all sorts, succeeded in full growth, maturity and perfection. On the FOURTH DAY, the two grand luminaries, the Sun and Moon, were created. The Sun to rule the day and the Moon to govern the night. And the sacred historian informs us that they were ordained for signs, seasons, days and years. The Almighty was also pleased to bespangle the ethereal concave of heaven with a multitude of stars, that man, whom he intended to make, might contemplate thereon, and justly admire his majesty and glory. On the FIFTH DAY, he caused the waters to bring forth a variety of fish for our use, and in order to imprint on the mind of man a reverential awe of his divine omnipotence, he created great whales, which, together with the other inhabitants of the mighty deep, multiplied exceedingly after their kind. On the same day, the Almighty caused the birds to fly in the air, that

The GLOBES, celestial and terrestial, are referred to in this section, and their uses explained. It need hardly be said that they are two artificial spherical bodies, on the convex surface of which are represented the countries, seas, and various parts of the earth, the face of the heavens, the planetary revolutions, and other particulars.

THE USE OF THE GLOBES.

Their principal use, besides serving as maps to distinguish the outward parts of the earth, and the situation of the fixed stars, is to illustrate and explain the phenomena arising from the annual revolution, and the diurnal rotation, of the earth round its own axis. They are valuable instruments for improving the mind, and giving it the most distinct idea of any problem

---

man might delight his eyes and ears with some for their beautiful plumage and others for their melodious notes.

On the *sixth day*, he created the beasts of the field and the reptiles which crawl on the earth. And here we may plainly perceive the wisdom, power and goodness of the Grand Geometrician of the Universe, made manifest throughout the whole of his proceedings. He produced what effects he pleased without the aid of their natural causes,—such as giving light to the world before he created the Sun and Moon, and making the earth fruitful without the influence of the heavenly bodies. He did not create the beasts of the field until he had provided sufficient herbage for their support, neither did he create man until he had furnished him with a dwelling, and everything requisite for life and pleasure. Then, to dignify the work of his hands still more, he made man, who came into the world with greater pomp than any creature which preceded him. They came but with a single command. God spake the word and it was done. But at the formation of man, we are told there was a consultation, in which God said, let us make man. He was immediately formed out of the dust of the earth. The breath of life was blown into his nostrils, and man became a living soul. In this one creature, there is a combination of every thing throughout the whole creation,—such as the quality and substance of an animate being, the life of plants, the senses of beasts ; but, above all, the understanding of angels ; formed after the immediate image of God, thereby intimating to him that integrity and uprightness should ever influence him to adore his Creator, who has so liberally bestowed on him the faculty of speech, and further endued him with that noble instinct called *reason*. The Almighty, as his last and best gift to man, created WOMAN. Under his forming hand the creature grew—manlike but of different sex—so lovely fair that what seemed fair in all the world, seemed now mean,—all in her summed up—in her contained. On she came, led by her heavenly maker, though unseen yet guided by his voice, adorned with all that heaven could bestow to make her amiable. "Grace was in all her steps, heaven in her eye, and in every gesture dignity and love."

The Almighty having finished the sixth day's work, rested on the SEVENTH. He blessed, hallowed and sanctified it. He thereby taught man to work industriously six days, but strictly commanded him to rest on the seventh, the better to contemplate on the beautiful works of creation—to adore him as their Creator—to go into his sanctuaries, and offer up praises for life and every blessing he so amply enjoys at his bountiful hands.

or proposition, as well as enabling it to solve the same. Contemplating these bodies, we are inspired with a due reverence for the Deity and his works, and are induced to encourage the studies of astronomy, geography, navigation, and the arts dependent on them, by which society has been so much benefited.

THE FIVE ORDERS OF ARCHITECTURE are introduced in this section, and severally illustrated. A brief description of them may not, therefore, be inappropriate in this place.

OF ORDER IN ARCHITECTURE.

By order in architecture, is meant a system of all the members, proportions and ornaments of columns and pilasters; or, it is a regular arrangement of the projecting parts of a building, which, united with those of a column, form a beautiful, perfect and complete whole.

OF ITS ANTIQUITY.

From the first formation of society, order in architecture may be traced. When the rigor of seasons first obliged men to contrive shelter from the inclemency of the weather, we learn that they planted trees on end, and then laid others across to support a covering. The bands, which connected those trees at top and bottom, are said to have given rise to the idea of the base and capital of pillars; and from this simple hint originally proceeded the more improved art of architecture.

The five orders are thus classed: the Tuscan, Doric, Ionic, Corinthian, Composite.

THE TUSCAN

Is the most simple and solid of the five orders. It was invented in Tuscany, whence it derives its name. Its column is seven diameters high; and its capital, base and entablature, have but few mouldings. The simplicity of the construction of this column, renders it eligible where ornament would be superfluous.

THE DORIC,

Which is plain and natural, is the most ancient, and was invented by the Greeks. Its column is eight diameters high, and has seldom any ornaments on base or capital, except mouldings; though the frieze is distinguished by triglyphs and metopes, and triglyphs compose the ornaments of the frieze. The solid composition of this order gives it a preference, in structures where strength and noble simplicity are chiefly required.

The Doric is the best proportioned of all the orders. The several parts, of which it is composed, are founded on the natural position of solid bodies. In its first invention it was more simple than in its present state. In after times, when it began to be adorned, it gained the name of Doric; for when it was constructed in its primitive and simple form, the name of Tuscan was conferred on it. Hence the Tuscan precedes the Doric in rank, on account of its resemblance to that pillar in its original state.

THE IONIC

Bears a kind of mean proportion between the more solid and delicate orders. Its column is nine diameters high; its capital is adorned with volutes, and its cornice has dentals. There are both delicacy and ingenuity displayed in this pillar; the invention of which is attributed to the Ionians, as the famous temple of Diana, at Ephesus, was of this order. It is said to have been formed after the model of an agreeable young woman of an elegant shape, dressed in her hair; in contrast to the Doric order, which was formed after that of a strong, robust man.

THE CORINTHIAN,

The richest of the five orders, is deemed a master-piece of art. Its column is ten diameters high, and its capital is adorned with two rows of leaves, and eight volutes, which sustain the abacus. The frieze is ornamented with curious devices, the cornice with dentals and modillions.

This order is used in stately and superb structures. It was invented at Corinth, by Callimachus, who is said to have taken the hint of the capital of this pillar from the following remarkable circumstance:—Accidentally passing by the tomb of a young lady, he perceived a basket of toys, covered with a tile, placed over an acanthus root,—it having been left there by her nurse. As the branches grew up, they compassed the basket, till arriving at the tile, they met with an obstruction, and bent downwards. Callimachus, struck with the object, set about imitating the figure: the vase of the capital he made to represent the basket; the abacus the tile; and the volutes the bending leaves.

THE COMPOSITE

Is compounded of the other orders, and was contrived by the Romans. Its capital has the two rows of leaves of the Corinthian, and the volutes of the Ionic. Its column has the quarter-round, as the Tuscan and Doric order; is ten diameters high, and its cornice has dentals, of simple modillions. This pillar is generally found in buildings where strength, elegance and beauty are displayed.

OF THE INVENTION OF ORDER IN ARCHITECTURE.

The ancient and original orders of architecture, esteemed by Masons, are no more than three—the *Doric, Ionic,* and *Corinthian,* which were invented by the Greeks. To these the Romans have added two: the Tuscan, which they made plainer than the Doric; and the Composite, which was more ornamental, if not more beautiful, than the Corinthian. The first three orders alone, however, shew invention and particular character, and essentially differ from each other; the two others have nothing but what is borrowed, and differ only accidentally: the Tuscan is the Doric in its earliest state; and the Composite is the Corinthian, enriched with the Ionic. To the Greeks, therefore, and not to the Romans, we are indebted for what is great, judicious and distinct in architecture.

THE FIVE SENSES OF HUMAN NATURE.

The intelligent Mason will readily understand the application of the following illustrations of the senses of HEARING, SEEING, FEELING, SMELLING and TASTING:

HEARING

Is that sense by which we distinguish sounds, and are capable of appreciating the agreeable charms of music. By it we are enabled to enjoy the pleasures of society, and reciprocally to communicate to each other our thoughts and intentions, our purposes and desires; and thus our reason is rendered capable of exerting its utmost power and energy.

The wise and beneficent Author of Nature intended, by the formation of this sense, that we should be social creatures, and receive the greatest and most important part of our knowledge from social intercourse with each other. For these purposes we are endowed with hearing, that by a proper exertion of our rational powers, our happiness may be complete.

SEEING

Is that sense by which we distinguish objects, and in an instant of time, without change of place or situation, view armies in battle array, figures of the most stately structures, and all the agreeable variety displayed in the landscape of nature. By this sense we find our way on the pathless ocean, traverse the globe of earth, determine its figure and dimensions, and delineate any region or quarter of it. By it we measure the planetary orbs, and make new discoveries in the sphere of the fixed stars. Nay, more: by it we perceive the tempers and dispositions, the passions and affections, of our fellow-creatures, when they wish most to conceal them; so that, though the tongue may be taught to lie and dissemble, the countenance will display the hypocrisy to the discerning eye. In fine, the rays of light which administer to this sense are the most astonishing parts of the animated creation, and render the eye a peculiar object of admiration.

Of all the faculties, sight is the noblest. The structure of the eye and its appurtenances, evinces the admirable contrivance of nature for performing all its various external and internal motions; while the variety displayed in the eyes of different animals, suited to their several ways of life, clearly demonstrates this organ to be the masterpiece of nature's works.

FEELING

Is that sense by which we distinguish the different qualities of bodies; such as heat and cold, hardness and softness, roughness and smoothness, figure, solidity, motion and extension.

These three senses, *Hearing*, *Seeing*, and *Feeling*, are deemed peculiarly essential among Masons.

SMELLING

Is that sense by which we distinguish odours, the various kinds of which convey different impressions to the mind. Animal and vegetable bodies, and indeed most other bodies, while exposed to the air, continually send forth effluvia of vast subtilty, as well in the state of life and growth, as in the state of fermentation and putrefaction. These effluvia, being drawn into the nostrils along with the air, are the means by which all bodies are smelled. Hence it is evident, that there is a manifest appearance of design in the great Creator's having planted the organ of smell in the inside of that canal, through which the air continually passes in respiration.

TASTING

Enables us to make a proper distinction in the choice of our food. The organ of this sense guards the entrance of the alimentary canal, as that of smelling guards the entrance of the canal for respiration. From the situation of both these organs, it is plain that they were intended by nature to distinguish wholesome food from that which is nauseous. Every thing that enters into the stomach must undergo the scrutiny of tasting; and by it we are capable of discerning the changes which the same body undergoes in the different compositions of art, cookery, chemistry, pharmacy, &c.

Smelling and tasting are inseparably connected; and it is by the unnatural kind of life men commonly lead in society, that these senses are rendered less fit to perform their natural offices.

OF THE SEVEN LIBERAL ARTS AND SCIENCES.

THE SEVEN LIBERAL ARTS AND SCIENCES are also illustrated in this section. A very brief analysis of the character of each may not therefore be altogether inappropriate in this place.

GRAMMAR

Is the key by which alone a door can be opened to the understanding of speech. It is Grammar which reveals the admirable art of language, and unfolds various constituent parts, its names, definitions, and respective offices: it unravels, as it were, the thread of which the web of speech is composed. These reflections seldom occur to any one before their acquaintance with the art; yet it is most certain, that, without a knowledge of Grammar, it is very difficult to speak with propriety, precision, and purity.

RHETORIC.

It is by Rhetoric that the art of speaking eloquently is acquired. To be an eloquent speaker, in the proper sense of the word, is far from being either a common, or an easy attainment: it is the art of being persuasive and commanding; the art, not only of pleasing the fancy, but of speaking both to the understanding and to the heart.

LOGIC

Is that science which directs us how to form clear and distinct ideas of things, and thereby prevents us from being misled by their similitude or resemblance. Of all the human sciences, that concerning man is certainly most worthy of man. The precise business of Logic is to explain the nature of the human mind, and the proper manner of conducting its several powers in the attainment of truth and knowledge. This science ought to be cultivated as the foundation or ground-work of our inquiries; particularly in the pursuit of those sublime principles, which claim our attention as Masons.

ARITHMETIC

Is the art of numbering, or that part of the mathematics which considers the properties of numbers in general. We have but a very imperfect idea of things without quantity, and as imperfect of quantity itself, without the help of Arithmetic. All the works of the Almighty are made in number, weight and measure; therefore, to understand them rightly, we ought to understand arithmetical calculations; and the greater advancement we make in the mathematical sciences, the more capable we shall be of considering such things as are the ordinary objects of our conceptions, and be thereby led to a more comprehensive knowledge of our great Creator, and the works of the creation.

GEOMETRY

Treats of the powers and properties of magnitudes in general, where length, breadth, and thickness are considered—from a *point* to a *line*, from a line to a *superficies*, and from a superfices to a *solid*.

A *point* is the beginning of all Geometrical matter.

A *line* is a continuation of the same.

A *superficies* is length and breadth without a given thickness.

A *solid* is length and breadth with a given thickness, which forms a cube and comprehends the whole.

OF THE ADVANTAGES OF GEOMETRY.

By this science, the architect is enabled to construct his plans, and execute his designs; the general, to arrange his soldiers; the engineer, to mark out grounds for encampments; the geographer, to give us the dimensions of the world, and all things therein contained, to delineate the extent of seas, and specify the divisions of empires, kingdoms and provinces. By it, also, the astronomer is enabled to make his observations, and to fix the duration of times and seasons, years and cycles. In fine, Geometry is the foundation of architecture, and the root of the mathematics.

MUSIC

Is that elevated science which affects the passions by sound. There are few who have not felt its charms, and acknowledged its expressions to be intelligible to the heart. It is a language of delightful sensations, far more elegant than words: it breathes to the ear the clearest intimations; it touches, and gently agitates the agreeable and sublime passions; it wraps us in melancholy, and elevates us in joy; it dissolves and enflames; it melts us in tenderness, and excites us to war. This science is truly congenial to the nature of man; for by its powerful charms, the most discordant passions may be harmonized and brought into perfect unison: but it never sounds with such seraphic harmony as when employed in singing hymns of gratitude to the Creator of the universe.

ASTRONOMY

Is that sublime science which inspires the contemplative vein to soar aloft, and read the wisdom, strength, and beauty of the great Creator in the heavens. How nobly eloquent of the Deity is the celestial hemisphere!—the most magnificent heralds of his infinite glory! They speak to the whole universe; for there is neither speech so barbarous, but their language is understood; nor nation so distant, but their voices are heard amongst them.

> The heavens proclaim the glory of God;
> The firmament declareth the works of his hands.

Assisted by Astronomy, we ascertain the laws which govern the heavenly bodies, and by which their motions are directed; investigate the power by which they circulate in their orbs, discover their size, determine their distance, explain their various phenomena, and correct the fallacy of the senses by the light of truth.

OF THE MORAL ADVANTAGES OF GEOMETRY.

Geometry, the first and noblest of sciences, is the basis on which the superstructure of Freemasonry is erected. By Geometry, we may curiously trace nature, through her various windings, to her most concealed recesses. By it, we discover the power, wisdom, and goodness, of the Grand Artificer of the Universe, and view with delight the proportions which connect this vast machine. By it, we discover how the planets move in their respective orbits, and demonstrate their various revolutions. By it, we account for the return of seasons, and the variety of scenes which each season displays to the discerning eye. Numberless worlds are around us, all framed by the same Divine Artist, which roll through the vast expanse, and are all conducted by the same unerring law of nature.

A survey of nature, and the observation of her beautiful proportions, first determined man to imitate the divine plan, and study symmetry and order. This gave rise to societies, and birth to every useful art. The architect began to design; and the plans which he laid down, being improved by experience and time, have produced works which are the admiration of every age.

The lapse of time, the ruthless hand of ignorance, and the devastations of war, have laid waste and destroyed many valuable monuments of antiquity, on which the utmost exertions of human genius have been employed. Even the Temple of Solomon, so spacious and magnificent, and constructed by so many celebrated artists, escaped not the unsparing ravages of barbarous force. Freemasonry, notwithstanding, has still survived. The *attentive ear* receives the sound from the *instructive tongue*, and the mysteries of Masonry are safely lodged in the repository of *faithful breasts*. Tools and implements of architecture are selected by the Fraternity, to imprint on the memory wise and serious truths; and thus, through a succession of ages, are transmitted unimpaired the most excellent tenets of our Institution.

CHARGE AT INITIATION INTO THE SECOND DEGREE.

My Brother:—Being advanced to the second degree of Freemasonry, I congratulate you on your preferment.

Masonry is a progressive moral science, divided into different degrees; and as its principles and mystic ceremonies are regularly developed and illustrated, it is intended and hoped that they will make a deep and lasting impression on the mind.

It is unnecessary to recapitulate the duties which, as a Fellow-Craft, you are bound to discharge. Your general good reputation affords satisfactory assurance, that you will not suffer any consideration to induce you to act in any manner unworthy the respectable character you now sustain. But, on the contrary, that you will ever display the discretion, the virtue, and the dignity, which become a worthy and exemplary Mason.

Our laws and regulations you are strenuously to support; and be always ready to assist in seeing them duly executed. You are not to palliate, or aggravate, the offences of your Brethren; but in the decision of every trespass against our rules, you are to judge with candor, admonish with friendship, and reprehend with justice.

The impressive ceremonies of this degree are calculated to inculcate upon the mind of the novitiate, the importance of the study of the liberal arts and sciences,—especially of the noble science of Geometry, which forms the basis of Freemasonry; and which, being of a divine and moral nature, is enriched with the most useful knowledge; for while it proves the wonderful properties of nature, it demonstrates the more important truths of morality. To the study of Geometry, therefore, your attention is specially directed.

Your past regular deportment and upright conduct have merited the honor we have conferred. In your present character, it is expected that at all our assemblies, you will observe the solemnities of our ceremonies,—that you will preserve the ancient usages and customs of the Fraternity sacred and inviolable,—and thus, by your example, induce others to hold them in due veneration.

Such is the nature of your engagements as a Fellow-Craft, and to a due observance of them, you are bound by the strongest ties of fidelity and honor.

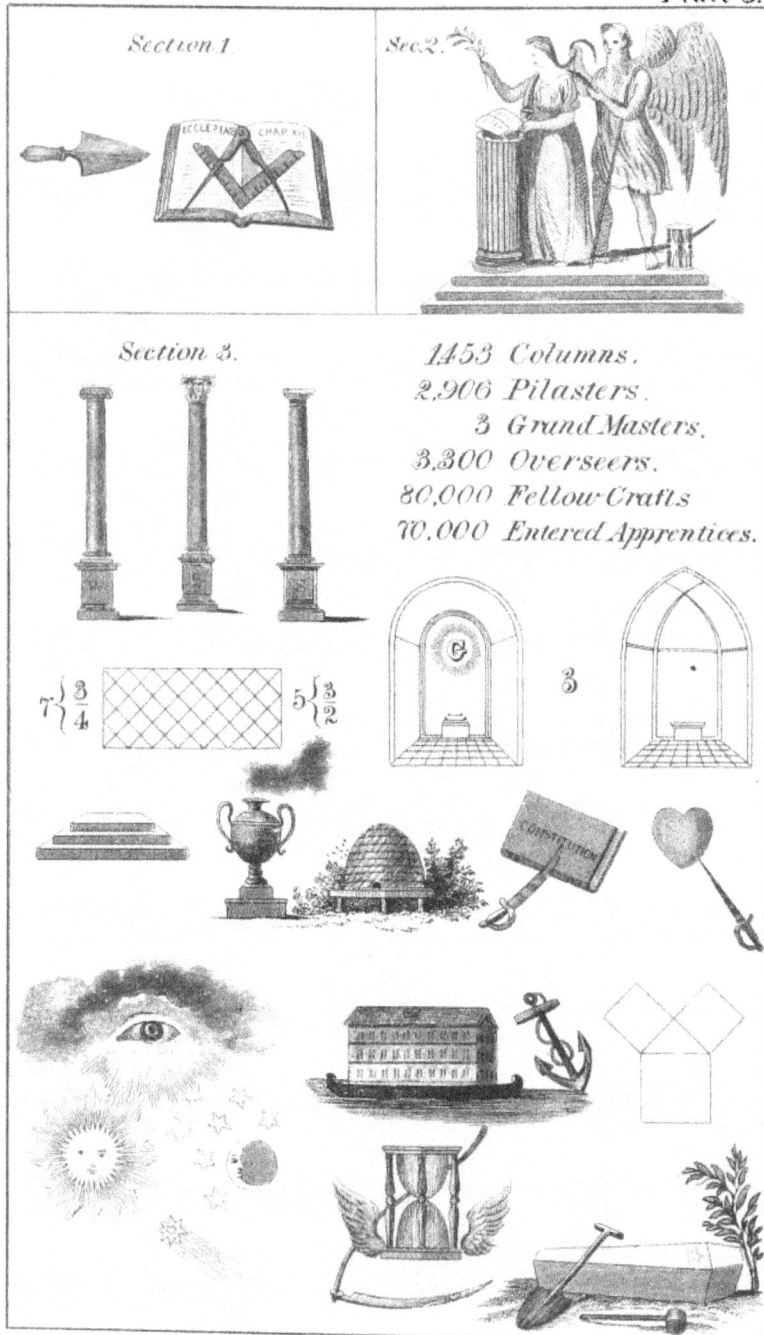

CHAPTER VIII.

REMARKS ON THE THIRD DEGREE.

As before remarked, Freemasonry in every degree is progressive. A knowledge of it can only be attained by time, patience, and application. In the first degree, we are taught the duties we owe to God, our neighbor and ourselves. In the second, we are more thoroughly inducted into the mysteries of moral science, and learn to trace the goodness and majesty of the Creator by minutely analyzing his works. But the third degree is the cement of the whole. It presents us with a series of historical facts and ceremonies, which illustrate many passages in the Jewish Scriptures, and refer to the fundamental truths of our holy religion. It is calculated to bind men together by mystic points of fellowship, as in a bond of fraternal affection and Brotherly Love. It is among Brethren of this degree, that the ancient landmarks of the Order are preserved, and it is from them that we derive that fund of information which none but ingenious and expert Masons can supply. It may be truly said, that but few ever attain to a perfect knowledge of it; yet it is not less true, that they who gain by merit the marks of preeminence and distinction which it confers, receive a reward which amply compensates them for their attention and assiduity.

It is also from Brethren of this degree, that the rulers of the Craft are selected; because it is only from those who are capable of giving instruction, that we can reasonably expect to receive it. And well would it be for our Lodges, and for the Fraternity at large, if the ancient regulation were more strictly observed, that no Brother should be permitted to be raised to this degree, who had not made himself thoroughly proficient in the two preceding.

Divested of those duties and ceremonies which more immediately appertain to the degree of a Past Master, this is divided into three sections, throughout the whole of which, we are taught to circumscribe our conduct within the boundary line of our duties to God and man.

FIRST SECTION.

The first section in this, as in the two preceding degrees, is initiatory; and a knowledge of it is indispensable to every Brother who is desirous of holding office, or who would make himself useful in the business-transactions of the Lodge.

The following passage of Scripture is introduced and read by the Master:—

"Remember now thy Creator in the days of thy youth, while the evil days come not, nor the years draw nigh, when thou shalt say, I have no pleasure in them; while the sun, or the light, or the moon, or the stars, be not darkened, nor the clouds return after the rain; in the day when the keepers of the house shall tremble, and the strong men shall bow themselves, and the grinders cease because they are few, and those that look out of the windows be darkened, and the doors shall be shut in the streets, when the sound of the grinding is low, and he shall rise up at the voice of the bird, and all the daughters of music shall be brought low. Also when they shall be afraid of that which is high, and fears shall be in the way, and the almond tree shall flourish, and the grasshopper shall be a burden, and desire shall fail; because man goeth to his long home, and the mourners go about the streets: or ever the silver cord be loosed, or the golden bowl be broken, or the pitcher be broken at the fountain, or the wheel broken at the cistern. Then shall the dust return to the earth as it was; and the spirit shall return unto God who gave it."—Ecclesiastes xii. 1—7.

All the implements in Masonry indiscriminately, properly belong to Brethren of this degree, and may be illustrated in this section. The TROWEL, however, is more particularly referred to.

THE TROWEL

Is an instrument made use of by operative Masons, to spread the cement which unites a building into one common mass; but we, as free and accepted Masons, are taught to make use of it for the more noble and glorious purpose of spreading the cement of Brotherly Love and affection; that cement which unites us into one sacred band, or society of friends and Brothers, among whom no contention should ever exist, but that noble contention, or rather emulation, of who best can work, and best agree.

SECOND SECTION.

This section recites the historical traditions of the Order, and presents to view a picture of great moral sublimity. It exemplifies an instance of virtue and firmness, seldom equalled, and never excelled.

REMARKS ON THE THIRD DEGREE.

PRAYER TO BE USED IN THE CEREMONY.

Almighty and Eternal God! Great Architect and Ruler of the Universe!—at whose creative fiat, all things first were made,—We, the frail creatures of thy Providence, humbly implore thee to pour down on this convocation, assembled in thy holy name, the continual dew of thy blessing. And we especially beseech thee to impart thy grace to this thy servant, who offers himself a candidate to partake with us the mysterious secrets of a Master Mason. Indue him with such fortitude that in the hour of trial he faint not; but pass him safely under thy protection, through the valley of the shadow of death, that he may finally arise from the tomb of transgression, and shine as the stars forever and ever. *Amen.*

Response. So mote it be.

THIRD SECTION.

This Section illustrates certain hieroglyphical emblems and inculcates many useful and impressive moral lessons. It also details many particulars relative to the building of the Temple at Jerusalem.

This magnificent structure was founded in the fourth year of the reign of Solomon, on the second day of the month Zif, being the second month of the sacred year. It was located on Mount Moriah, near the place where Abraham was about to offer up his son Isaac, and where David met and appeased the destroying angel. Josephus informs us, that although more than seven years were occupied in building it, yet, during the whole term it did not rain in the day time, that the workmen might not be obstructed in their labor. From sacred history we also learn, that there was not the sound of axe, hammer or any tool of iron, heard in the house while it was building.

It is said to have been supported by fourteen hundred and fifty-three columns, and two thousand nine hundred and six pilasters; all hewn from the finest Parian marble. There were employed in its building three Grand Masters; three thousand and three hundred Masters, or Overseers of the Work; eighty thousand Fellow-Crafts; and seventy thousand Entered Apprentices, or bearers of burthens. All these were classed and arranged in such manner by the wisdom of Solomon, that neither envy, discord, nor confusion, were suffered to interrupt or disturb the peace and good fellowship which prevailed among the workmen.

In front of the magnificent porch, were placed the two celebrated pillars,—one on the left hand and one on the right hand. They are supposed to have been placed there as a memorial to the children of Israel of the happy deliverance of their forefathers from Egyptian bondage, and in commemoration of the miraculous pillars of fire and cloud. The pillar of fire gave light to the Israelites and facilitated their march, and the cloud proved darkness to Pharaoh and his host and retarded their pursuit. King Solomon, therefore, ordered these pillars to be placed at the entrance of the Temple, as the most conspicuous part, that the children of Israel might have that happy event continually before their eyes, in going to and returning from divine worship.

In this section are also explained a variety of appropriate emblems, with which the skilful Brother will not fail to make himself familiarly acquainted. Among them are the following :

THE POT OF INCENSE

Is an emblem of a pure heart, which is always an acceptable sacrifice to the Deity ; and as this glows with fervent heat, so should our hearts continually glow with gratitude to the great and beneficent Author of our existence, for the manifold blessings and comforts we enjoy.

THE BEE-HIVE

Is an emblem of industry, and recommends the practice of that virtue to all created beings, from the highest seraph in heaven to the lowest reptile of the dust. It teaches us that as we came into the world rational and intelligent beings, so we should ever be industrious ones ; never sitting down contented, while our fellow-creatures around us are in want ; especially when it is in our power to relieve them, without inconvenience to ourselves.

When we take a survey of nature, we view man, in his infancy, more helpless and indigent than the brutal creation: he lies languishing for days, months and years, totally incapable of providing sustenance for himself, of guarding against the attacks of the wild beasts of the field, or sheltering himself from the inclemencies of the weather.

It might have pleased the great Creator of heaven and earth to have made man independent of all other beings; but, as dependence is one of the strongest bonds of society, mankind were made dependent on each other for protection and security ; as they thereby enjoy better opportunities of fulfilling the duties of reciprocal love and friendship. Thus was man formed for social and active life, the noblest part of the work of God ; and he that will so demean himself as not to be endeavoring to add to the common stock of knowledge and understanding, may be deemed a *drone* in the *hive* of nature, a useless member of society, and unworthy of our protection as Masons.

THE BOOK OF CONSTITUTIONS, GUARDED BY THE TYLER'S SWORD,

Reminds us that we should be ever watchful and guarded, in our thoughts, words and actions, particularly when before the enemies of Masonry ; ever bearing in remembrance those truly Masonic virtues, *silence* and *circumspection.*

THE SWORD, POINTING TO A NAKED HEART,

Demonstrates that justice will sooner or later overtake us; and although our thoughts, words and actions, may be hidden from the eyes of man, yet that

ALL-SEEING EYE,

Whom the SUN, MOON and STARS obey, and under whose watchful care even COMETS perform their stupendous revolutions, pervades the inmost recesses of the human heart, and will reward us according to our merits.

THE ANCHOR AND ARK

Are emblems of a well grounded *hope,* and a well spent life. They are emblematical of that divine *ark* which safely wafts us over this tempestuous sea of troubles, and that *anchor* which shall safely moor us in a peaceful harbor, where the wicked cease from troubling, and the weary shall find rest.

THE FORTYSEVENTH PROBLEM OF EUCLID.

This was an invention of the ancient philosopher, the great Pythagoras, who, in his travels through Asia, Africa and Europe, was initiated into several orders of Priesthood, and is said to have been raised to the sublime degree of a Master Mason. This wise philosopher enriched his mind abundantly in a general knowledge of things, and more especially in Geometry, or Masonry. On this subject, he drew out many problems and theorems; and among the most distinguished he erected this, which, in the joy of his heart, he called *Eureka,* in the Grecian language, signifying, *I have found it;* and upon the discovery of which, he is said to have sacrificed a hecatomb. It teaches Masons to be general lovers of the arts and sciences.

THE HOUR-GLASS

Is an emblem of human life. Behold! how swiftly the sands run, and how rapidly our lives are drawing to a close. We cannot without astonishment behold the little particles which are contained in this machine, how they pass away almost imperceptibly, and yet to our surprise, in the short space of an hour, they are all exhausted. Thus wastes man! to-day, he puts forth the tender leaves of hope; to-morrow, blossoms, and bears his blushing honors thick upon him; the next day comes a frost, which nips the shoot, and when he thinks his greatness is still aspiring, he falls, like autumn leaves, to enrich our mother earth.

THE SCYTHE

Is an emblem of time, which cuts the brittle thread of life, and launches us into eternity. Behold! what havock the scythe of time makes among the human race: if by chance we should escape the numerous evils incident to childhood and youth, and with health and vigor arrive to the years of manhood, yet withal we must soon be cut down by the all-devouring Scythe of time, and be gathered into the land where our fathers have gone before us.

THE THREE STEPS,

Usually delineated upon the Master's Carpet, are emblematical of the three principal stages of human life, viz: youth, manhood, and age. In youth, as Entered Apprentices, we ought industriously to occupy our minds in the attainment of useful knowledge: in manhood, as Fellow-Crafts, we should apply our knowledge to the discharge of our respective duties to God, our neighbor, and ourselves; that so in age, as Master Masons, we may enjoy the happy reflections consequent on a well spent life, and die in the hope of a glorious immortality.

CHARGE AT INITIATION INTO THE THIRD DEGREE.

MY BROTHER—Your zeal for our Institution, the progress you have made in our mystery, and your steady conformity to our useful regulations, have pointed you out as a proper object for this peculiar mark of our favor.

Duty and honor, now alike bind you to be faithful to every trust; to support the dignity of your character on all occasions; and strenuously to enforce, by precept and example, a steady obedience to the tenets of Freemasonry. Exemplary conduct on your part will convince the world, that merit is the just title to our privileges, and that on you our favors are not undeservedly bestowed.

In this respectable character, you are authorized to correct the irregularities of your less informed Brethren; to fortify their minds with resolution against the snares of the insidious, and to guard them against every allurement to vicious practices. To preserve unsullied the reputation of the Fraternity, ought to be your constant care; and, therefore, it becomes your province to caution the inexperienced against a breach of fidelity. To your inferiors in rank or office, you are to recommend obedience and submission; to your equals, courtesy and affability; to your superiors, kindness and condescension. Universal benevolence you are zealously to inculcate; and by the regularity of your own conduct, endeavor to remove every aspersion against this venerable Institution. Our ancient land-marks you are carefully to preserve, and not suffer them, on any pretence, to be infringed, or countenance a deviation from our established customs.

Your honor and reputation are concerned in supporting with dignity, the respectable character you now bear. Let no motive, therefore, make you swerve from your duty, violate your vows, or betray your trust; but be true and faithful, and imitate the example of that celebrated artist whom you have this evening represented. Thus you will render yourself deserving of the honor which we have conferred, and worthy of the confidence that we have reposed.

CHAPTER IX.

REMARKS ON THE PRESENT, OR PAST MASTER'S DEGREE.

This degree is usually classed as the *fifth* in order; which arrangement carries it into a foreign organization, independent of the authority of the Grand Lodges. It is not, however, necessarily connected with any other than the symbolic degrees. It therefore more properly follows as the *fourth* in order.

It is an honorary degree, and has neither a written nor traditional history. Unlike every other degree in Freemasonry, it sheds no light upon itself. That none but Brethren equally distinguished for their intellectual endowments and great professional skill, were anciently selected to preside as Masters of Lodges, does not admit of a question. At the time of the introduction of the Order into Europe, the Presiding Masters were the Chief Overseers of the work. At a subsequent period, they were the only legal representatives in the general assemblies of the Craft. They constituted a distinct class or order. We learn from the preceding degrees that each class or division of the workmen at the Temple, had their own peculiar and appropriate tests of recognition—as the Apprentices and Craftsmen. Is it unreasonable to infer that the Presiding Masters had theirs also?

The tradition of one of the degrees informs us, that the workmen at the Temple, were divided into companies or Lodges, (some Masonic writers say of thirtysix members,) at the head of each of which was placed an *Overseer*; and there were employed in that great work three hundred Herodim, or *Masters*, to whom the Overseers were themselves subordinate.*

This organization continued until after the completion of the Temple, when it was no longer either useful or practicable. The time

---
*Vide Calcott's Masonry, page 66.

had then arrived when the vast number of men engaged in that great work, were to disperse and seek employment elsewhere. We know, however, that a portion of them still continued in the service of Solomon, and that they built a splendid palace for his own use, another for his Egyptian Queen, and a third for an occasional residence. They surrounded Jerusalem with walls,—built the celebrated arsenal and senate chamber called Millo,—fortified a number of towns on the frontiers, and in the centre of his dominions. They also built Palmyra and Baalbec, between the Euphrates and the coast, and Gezer and lower Beth-horon, between Joppa and the Red Sea, together with the store cities and store houses on the east and west of the Jordan. Another portion of them were employed by Hiram in beautifying his own city of Tyre. Still another portion travelled into foreign countries; and we trace them through Asia Minor into Assyria, Medea, Persia, India, Arabia, Egypt, and other parts of Great Asia, and into Africa and Europe.

As we have already suggested, when this dispersion took place, the organization instituted by Solomon was, from the necessity of the case, in a measure broken up. The Overseers, who had been subject to the three hundred Masters, were now, with their respective companies, or Lodges, thrown upon their own resources, and upon their own independent government. They, in their turn, became Presiding Masters, and appointed their own Overseers, or Wardens. As their Masters had been furnished by Solomon with the means of recognition, a similar measure would naturally suggest itself to their minds,—especially as they were about to separate and disperse themselves over the whole world. Or, this arrangement may have taken place through the agency of Solomon, and the three hundred Herodim, as a reward for their fidelity. On the breaking up of the Temple-organization, the Grand Master may have instituted this degree, and created Lodges for Presiding Masters. But whatever the origin of the degree may have been, its tendency is to strengthen the bonds which bind one Brother to another; and wherever Past Masters may be dispersed, or however reduced in circumstances, they will always meet with a Brother's welcome and a Brother's sympathy, at the hands of Presiding Masters.

The degree should be carefully studied and well understood by every Master of a Lodge, the duties appertaining to whose responsible station are many and various—embracing the whole range of Masonic labors from the Apprentice to the Master—including the Opening and Closing of Lodges—the Initiating, Crafting and Raising of Masons,—the forms of Installation and Consecration, in Grand as well as subordinate Lodges—the ceremonies of Laying the Corner-Stones of public edifices—of forming and conducting Processions—the Constitution of new Lodges—the Dedication of Masonic Halls—the Conducting of Funeral Ceremonies and services,—with all the detail that go to make up these general duties, and which are particularly set forth in the following sections.

FIRST SECTION.

OF THE MANNER OF CONSTITUTING A LODGE.

Any number of Master Masons, not under seven, desirous of forming a new Lodge, must apply, by petition, to the Grand Lodge of the State in which they reside, as follows :—

FORM OF A PETITION FOR A NEW LODGE.

"*To the Most Worshipful Grand Lodge of the State of* ———.

The undersigned petitioners, being ancient Free and Accepted Master Masons, having the prosperity of the Fraternity at heart, and willing to exert their best endeavors to promote and diffuse the genuine principles of Masonry, respectfully represent—

"That for the convenience of their respective dwellings, and for other good reasons, they are desirous of forming a new Lodge in the town of ——— to be named ———. They therefore pray for letters of dispensation, or a warrant of constitution, to empower them to assemble, as a legal Lodge, to discharge the duties of Masonry, in a regular and constitutional manner, according to the original forms of the Order, and the regulations of the Grand Lodge. They have nominated and do recommend Brother A. B. to be the first Master; C. D. to be the first Senior Warden, and E. F. to be the first Junior Warden, of said Lodge. If the prayer of the petition shall be granted, they promise a strict conformity to all the constitutions, laws and regulations of the Grand Lodge."

This petition being signed by at least seven regular Masons, and recommended by a Lodge, or Lodges, adjacent to the place where the new Lodge is to be holden, is delivered to the Grand Secretary, who lays it before the Grand Lodge.

If the petition meets the approbation of the Grand Lodge, a Dispensation is ordered to be issued, which is signed by the Grand or

Deputy Grand Master, and authorizes the petitioners to assemble as a *legal* Lodge, for a specified time.

Lodges working under Dispensations are considered merely as agents of the Grand Lodge. Their presiding officers are not entitled to the rank of Past Masters; nor are their officers privileged with a vote or voice in the Grand Lodge. The officers cannot be changed without the special approbation and appointment of the Grand Lodge; and in case of the cessation of such Lodges, their funds, jewels, and other property, accumulated by initiations into the several degrees, become the property of the Grand Lodge, and must be delivered over to the Grand Treasurer.

When Lodges, which are at first instituted by Dispensation, have passed a proper term of probation, they make application to the Grand Lodge for a Charter of Constitution. If this be obtained, the Grand Master appoints a day and hour for constituting and consecrating the new Lodge, and for installing its Master, Wardens, and other officers.

If the Grand Master, in person, attends the ceremony, the Lodge is said to be constituted in *ample form*; if the Deputy Grand Master only, it is said to be constituted in *due form*; but if the power of performing the ceremony is vested in a subordinate Lodge, it is said to be constituted in *form*.

CEREMONY OF CONSTITUTION.

On the day and hour appointed, the Grand Master and his officers meet in a convenient room, near to that in which the Lodge to be constituted is assembled, and open the Grand Lodge in the three degrees of Masonry.

The officers of the new Lodge are to be examined by the Deputy Grand Master, after which they return to their Lodge.

The new Lodge then sends a messenger to the Grand Master with the following message, viz:

" Most Worshipful,

The officers and Brethren of ——— Lodge, who are now assembled at ———, have instructed me to inform you, that the Most Worshipful Grand Lodge (or Grand Master) was pleased to grant them a letter of Dispensation, bearing date the ——— day of ———, in the year ———, authorizng them to form and open a Lodge of Free and Accepted Masons, in the town of ———; that since that period they have regularly assembled, and

CEREMONY OF CONSTITUTION.

conducted the business of Masonry according to the best of their abilities; that their proceedings, having received the approbation of the Most Worshipful Grand Lodge, they have obtained a Charter of constitution, and are desirous that their Lodge should be consecrated, and their officers installed, agreeably to the ancient usages and customs of the Craft; for which purpose they are now met, and await the pleasure of the Most Worshipful Grand Master."

He then returns to his Lodge, who prepare for the reception of the Grand Lodge. When notice is given that they are prepared, the Grand Lodge walk in procession to their hall. When the Grand Master enters, the grand honors are given by the new Lodge; the officers of which resign their seats to the grand officers, and take their several stations on their left.

The necessary cautions are then given, and all, excepting Masters and Past Masters of Lodges, are requested to retire, until the Master of the new Lodge is placed in the Oriental Chair. He is then bound to the faithful performance of his trust, and duly invested.

Upon due notice, the Grand Marshal reconducts the Brethren into the hall, and all take their places, except the members of the new Lodge, who form a procession on one side of the hall, to salute their Master. As they advance, the Grand Master addresses them, "*Brethren, behold your Master!*" As they pass, they make the proper salutation; and when they have all passed, he joins them, and takes his appropriate station.

A grand procession is then formed, in the following order, viz:

Tyler, with a Drawn Sword;
Two Stewards, with White Rods;
Entered Apprentices;
Fellow-Crafts;
Master Masons;
Stewards;
Junior Deacons;
Senior Deacons;
Secretaries;
Treasurers;
Past Wardens;
Junior Wardens;
Senior Wardens;
[Mark Masters;]
Past Masters;
Royal Arch Masons;

Knights Templars ;
Masters of Lodges.

THE NEW LODGE.

Tyler, with a Drawn Sword ;
Stewards, with White Rods ;
Entered Apprentices ;
Fellow-Crafts ;
Master Masons ;
Deacons ;
Secretary and Treasurer ;
Two Brethren, carrying the Lodge ;*
Junior and Senior Wardens ;
The Holy Writings, carried by the Oldest Member, not in office ;
The Master ;
Music.

THE GRAND LODGE.

Grand Tyler, with a Drawn Sword ;
Grand Stewards, with White Rods ;
A Brother, carrying a Golden Vessel of Corn ;†
Two Brethren, carrying Silver Vessels, one of Wine, the other of Oil ;
Grand Secretaries ;
Grand Treasurer ;
A Burning Taper, borne by a Past Master ;
A Past Master, bearing the Holy Writings ;
Square and Compass supported by two Stewards with Rods ;
Two Burning Tapers, borne by two Past Masters ;
Clergy and Orator ;
The Tuscan and Composite Orders ;
The Doric, Ionic and Corinthian Orders ;
Past Grand Wardens ;
Past Deputy Grand Masters ;
Past Grand Masters ;
The Globes ;
Junior and Senior Grand Wardens ;
Right Worshipful Deputy Grand Master ;
The Master of the Oldest Lodge, carrying the Book of Constitutions ;
The M. W. GRAND MASTER ;
The Grand Deacons, on a line seven feet apart, on the right and left of the
Grand Master, with Black Rods ;
Grand Sword Bearer, with a Drawn Sword ;
Two Stewards, with White Rods.

The procession moves on to the church or house where the services are to be performed. When the front of the procession arrives

---

*Flooring. †Wheat.

CEREMONY OF CONSTITUTION. 51

at the door, they halt, open to the right and left, and face inward, while the Grand Master, and others, in succession, pass through and enter the house.

A platform is erected in front of the pulpit, and provided with seats for the accommodation of the grand officers.

The Bible, Square and Compass, and Book of Constitutions, are placed upon a table, in front of the Grand Master; the *Lodge* is placed in the centre, upon the platform, covered with white satin or linen, and encompassed by the three tapers, and the vessels of corn, wine and oil.

A piece of music is performed, and the public services commence with prayer. An oration, or sermon, upon the design and principles of the Institution, is then delivered by the Grand Chaplain, or some one appointed for that purpose, which is succeeded by a piece of music. The Grand Marshal then directs the officers and members of the new Lodge to form in front of the Grand Master. The Deputy Grand Master addresses the Grand Master, as follows:

"Most Worshipful,

"A number of Brethren, duly instructed in the mysteries of Masonry, having assembled together at stated periods, for some time past, by virtue of a Dispensation granted them for that purpose, do now desire to be *constituted* into a *regular Lodge*, agreeably to the ancient usages and customs of the Fraternity."

Their Secretary then delivers the Dispensation and records to the Master Elect, who presents them to the Grand Master.

The Grand Master examines the records, and if they are found correct, proclaims,

"The records appear to be properly entered, and are approved. Upon due deliberation, the Grand Lodge have granted the Brethren of this new Lodge a Charter, confirming them in the rights and privileges of a *regularly constituted Lodge:* which the Grand Secretary will now read."

After the Charter is read, the Grand Master then says,

"We shall now proceed, according to ancient usage, to constitute these Brethren into a regular Lodge."

Whereupon the several officers of the new Lodge deliver up their jewels and badges to *their* Master, who presents them, with his own, to the Deputy Grand Master, and he to the Grand Master.

The Deputy Grand Master now presents the Master Elect of the new Lodge, to the Grand Master, saying,

"Most Worshipful,
"I present you Brother ———, whom the members of the Lodge now to be constituted have chosen for their Master."

The Grand Master asks them if they remain satisfied with their choice. *(They bow in token of assent.)*

The Master then presents, severally, his Wardens, and other officers, naming them and their respective offices. The Grand Master asks the Brethren if they remain satisfied with each and all of them. *(They bow as before.)*

The officers and members of the new Lodge then form in the broad aisle, in front of the Grand Master; and the business of consecration commences with solemn music.

CEREMONY OF CONSECRATION.

The Grand Master, attended by the grand officers, and the Grand Chaplain, form themselves in order, round the Lodge, which is then uncovered, while a piece of solemn music is performed. The first clause of the Consecration Prayer is then rehearsed, as follows, the Brethren kneeling, viz:

"Great Architect of the Universe! Maker and Ruler of all Worlds! deign, from thy celestial temple, from realms of light and glory, to bless us in all the purposes of our present assembly!

"We humbly invoke thee to give us, at this and at all times, *Wisdom* in all our doings, *Strength* of mind in all our difficulties, and the *Beauty* of harmony in all our communications!

"Permit us, O thou Author of Light and Life, great Source of Love and Happiness, to erect this Lodge, and now solemnly to *consecrate* it to the honor of thy glory!

"*Glory be to God on high.*"

[Response by the Brethren.]

"*As it was in the beginning, is now, and ever shall be! Amen.*"

During the response, the Deputy Grand Master, and the Grand Wardens take the vessels of corn, wine, and oil, and sprinkle the elements of Consecration upon the Lodge.

[*The Grand Chaplain then continues:*]

"Grant, O Lord our God, that those who are now about to be invested with the government of this Lodge, may be endued with wisdom to instruct their Brethren in all their duties. May *Brotherly Love*, *Relief* and *Truth*, always prevail amongst the members of this Lodge; and may this bond of union continue to strengthen the Lodges throughout the world!

"Bless all our Brethren, wherever dispersed: and grant speedy relief to all who are either oppressed or distressed.

"We affectionately commend to thee all the members of thy whole family. May they increase in the knowledge of thee, and in the love of each other.

"Finally; May we finish all our work here below with thine approbation; and then have our transition from this earthly abode to thy heavenly temple above, there to enjoy light, glory and bliss, ineffable and eternal!

"*Glory be to God on high!*"

[Response by the Brethren.]

"*As it was in the beginning, is now, and ever shall be!
Amen! so mote it be! Amen!*"

Then succeeds solemn music, while the Lodge is covered. The Grand Chaplain then DEDICATES the Lodge, in the following terms:

"To the memory of HOLY SAINT JOHN, we Dedicate this Lodge. May every Brother revere his character, and imitate his virtues.

"*Glory be to God on high!*"

[Response.]

"*As it was in the beginning, is now, and ever shall be, world without end!
"Amen,! so mote it be! Amen!*"

A piece of music is then performed, whilst the Brethren of the new Lodge advance in procession to salute the Grand Lodge, with their hands crossed upon their breast, and bowing as they pass. They then take their places, and stand as they were.

The Grand Master then rises, and constitutes the new Lodge in the form following:

"In the name of the Most Worshipful Grand Lodge, I now constitute and form you, my good Brethren, into a Lodge of Free and Accepted Masons. From henceforth I empower you to act as a regular Lodge, constituted in conformity to the rites of our Order, and the charges of our ancient and honorable Fraternity; and may the Supreme Architect of the Universe prosper, direct and counsel you in all your doings."

[Response by all the Brethren.]

"*So mote it be!*"

The following, or some other Hymn, may then be sung :—

[By Brother St. John Phillips.]

Thou! who art God alone,
Accept before thy Throne
   Our fervent pray'r!
To fill with light and grace
This House, thy dwelling-place,
And bless thy chosen race,
   O God! draw near!

As through the universe,
All nature's works diverse,
   Thy praise accord;
Let Faith upon us shine,
And Charity combine,
With Hope, to make us thine,
   Jehovah, Lord!

Spirit of Truth and Love!
Descending from above,
   Our hearts inflame:
Till Masonry's control,
Shall build in one the whole,
A temple of the soul,
   To thy great Name!

SECOND SECTION.

CEREMONY OF INSTALLATION.

The Grand Master* asks his Deputy, "Whether he has examined the Master nominated in the warrant, and finds him well skilled in the noble science and the royal art." The Deputy answering in the affirmative,† by the Grand Master's order, takes the candidate from among his fellows, and presents him at the pedestal saying, "Most Worshipful Grand Master, I present my worthy Brother, A. B., to be Installed Master of this new Lodge. I find him to be of good morals, and of great skill, true and trusty; and as he is a lover of the whole Fraternity, wheresoever dispersed over the face of the earth, I doubt not he will discharge his duty with fidelity,"

---

*In this and other similar instances, where the Grand Master is specified in acting, may be understood any Master who performs the ceremony.

†A private examination is understood to precede the Installation of every officer.

The Grand Master then addresses him:

"BROTHER,

"Previous to your investiture, it is necessary that you should signify your assent to those ancient charges and regulations which point out the duty of a Master of a Lodge."

The Grand Master then reads, or orders to be read, a summary of the Ancient Charges to the Master elect, as follows, viz:

"I. You agree to be a good man and true, and strictly to obey the moral law.

"II. You agree to be a peaceable citizen, and cheerfully to conform to the laws of the country in which you reside.

"III. You promise not to be concerned in plots and conspiracies against government, but patiently to submit to the decisions of the supreme Legislature.

"IV. You agree to pay a proper respect to the civil magistrate, to work diligently, live creditably, and act honorably by all men.

"V. You agree to hold in veneration the original rulers and patrons of the order of Masonry, and their regular successors, supreme and subordinate, according to their stations; and to submit to the awards and resolutions of your Brethren, when convened, in every case consistent with the constitutions of the Order.

"VI. You agree to avoid private piques and quarrels, and to guard against intemperance and excess.

"VII. You agree to be cautious in carriage and behaviour, courteous to your Brethren and faithful to your Lodge.

"VIII. You promise to respect genuine Brethren, and to discountenance impostors, and all dissenters from the original plan of Masonry.

"IX. You agree to promote the general good of society, to cultivate the social virtues, and to propagate the knowledge of the art.

"X. You promise to pay homage to the Grand Master for the time being, and to his officers when duly installed; and strictly to conform to every edict of the Grand Lodge, or General Assembly of Masons, that is not subversive of the principles and ground work of Masonry.

"XI. You admit that it is not in the power of any man, or body of men to make innovations in the body of Masonry.

"XII. You promise a regular attendance on the committees and communications of the Grand Lodge, on receiving proper notice; and to pay attention to all the duties of Masonry, on convenient occasions.

"XIII. You admit that no new Lodge shall be formed without permission of the Grand Lodge: and that no countenance be given to any irregular Lodge, or to any person clandestinely initiated therein, being contrary to the ancient charges of the Order.

"XIV. You admit that no person can be regularly made a Mason in, or admitted a member of, any regular Lodge, without previous notice, and due inquiry into his character.

"XV. You agree that no visiters shall be received into your Lodge without due examination, and producing proper vouchers of their having been initiated in a regular Lodge."

These are the regulations of Free and Accepted Masons.

The Grand Master then addresses the Master Elect in the following manner : " Do you submit to these charges, and promise to support these regulations, as Masters have done in all ages before you ?" The new Master having signified his cordial submission as before, the Grand Master thus addresses him :

"Brother A. B., in consequence of your cheerful conformity to the charges and regulations of the Order, you are now to be Installed Master of this new Lodge, in full confidence of your care, skill and capacity to govern the same."

The new Master is then regularly invested with the insignia of his office, and the furniture and implements of his Lodge.

The various implements of the profession are emblematical of our conduct in life, and upon this occasion are carefully enumerated.

"The *Holy Writings*, that great light in Masonry, will guide you to all truth ; it will direct your paths to the temple of happiness, and point out to you the whole duty of man.

"The *Square* teaches us to regulate our actions by rule and line, and to harmonize our conduct by the principles of morality and virtue.

"The *Compass* teaches us to limit our desires in every station, that, rising to eminence by merit, we may live respected, and die regretted.

"The *Rule* directs, that we should punctually observe our duty ; press forward in the path of virtue, and, neither inclining to the right nor to the left, in all our actions have *eternity* in view.

"The *Line* teaches us the criterion of moral rectitude, to avoid dissimulation in conversation and action, and to direct our steps to the path which leads to *immortality*.

"The *Book of Constitutions* you are to search at all times. Cause it be read in your Lodge, that none may pretend ignorance of the excellent precepts it enjoins.

"You now receive in charge the *Charter*, by the authority of which this Lodge is held. You are carefully to preserve and duly transmit it to your successor in office.

"Lastly, you receive in charge the *By-Laws* of your Lodge, which you are to see carefully and punctually executed."

The Jewels of the officers of the new Lodge, are then returned to the Master, who delivers them, respectively, to the several officers of the Grand Lodge, according to their rank.

The subordinate officers of the new Lodge are then invested with their jewels, by the grand officers of corresponding rank ; and are by them, severally in turn, conducted to the Grand Master, who delivers to each of them a short charge, as follows, viz :

CEREMONY OF INSTALLATION. 57

THE SENIOR WARDEN.

"Brother C. D., you are appointed* Senior Warden of this new Lodge, and are now invested with the ensign of your office.

"The *Level* demonstrates that we are descended from the same stock, partake of the same nature, and share the same hope; and though distinctions among men are necessary to preserve subordination, yet no eminence of station should make us forget that we are Brethren; for he who is placed on the lowest spoke of fortune's wheel, may be entitled to our regard; because a time will come, and the wisest knows not how soon, when all distinction, but that of goodness, shall cease; and death, the grand leveler of human greatness, reduce us to the same state.

"Your regular attendance on our stated meetings is essentially necessary. In the absence of the Master, you are to govern this Lodge; in his presence, you are to assist him in the government of it. I firmly rely on your knowledge of Masonry, and attachment to the Lodge, for the faithful discharge of the duties of this important trust.—*Look well to the West!*"

THE JUNIOR WARDEN.

"Brother E. F., you are appointed Junior Warden of this new Lodge; and are now invested with the badge of your office.

"The *Plumb* admonishes us to walk uprightly in our several stations, to hold the scale of justice in equal poise, to observe the just medium between intemperance and pleasure, and to make our passions and prejudices coincide with the line of our duty.

"To you is committed the superintendence of the Craft during the hours of refreshment; it is therefore indispensably necessary, that you should not only be temperate and discreet, in the indulgence of your own inclinations, but carefully observe that none of the Craft be suffered to convert the means of refreshment into intemperance and excess.

"Your regular and punctual attendance is particularly requested; and I have no doubt that you will faithfully execute the duty which you owe to your present appointment.—*Look well to the South!*"

THE TREASURER.

"Brother G. H., you are appointed Treasurer of this new Lodge. It is your duty to receive all monies from the hands of the Secretary, keep just and regular accounts of the same, and pay them out at the Worshipful Master's will and pleasure, with the consent of the Lodge. I trust, your regard for the Fraternity will prompt you to the faithful discharge of the duties of your office.

THE SECRETARY.

"Brother I. K., you are appointed Secretary of this new Lodge. It is your duty to observe the Worshipful Master's will and pleasure, to record the proceedings of the Lodge, to receive all monies, and pay them into the hands of the Treasurer.

"Your good inclination to Masonry and this Lodge, I hope, will induce you to discharge your office with fidelity, and by so doing, you will merit the esteem and applause of your Brethren."

---

*When the Installation is not of the officers of a new Lodge, the words "have been elected," should be substituted for the words "are appointed," in all cases where the officer is chosen by ballot.

THE SENIOR AND JUNIOR DEACONS.

"Brothers L. M. and N. O., you are appointed Deacons of this new Lodge. It is your province to attend on the Master and Wardens, and to act as their proxies in the active duties of the Lodge; such as in the reception of candidates into the different degrees of Masonry; the introduction and accommodation of visiters, and in the immediate practice of our rites. These Rods, as badges of your office, I entrust to your care, not doubting your vigilance and attention."

THE STEWARDS.

"Brothers P. Q. and R. S., you are appointed Stewards of this new Lodge. The duties of your office are, to assist in the collection of dues and subscriptions, to keep an account of the Lodge expenses, to see that the tables are properly furnished at refreshment. and that every Brother is suitably provided for: and generally to assist the Deacons and other officers in performing their respective duties. Your regular and early attendance will afford the best proof of your zeal and attachment to the Lodge."

THE TYLER.

"Brother T. U., you are appointed Tyler of this Lodge, and I invest you with the implement of your office. As the sword is placed in the hands of the Tyler, to enable him effectually to guard against the approach of cowans and evesdroppers, and suffer none to pass or repass but such as are duly qualified; so it should admonish us to set a guard over our thoughts, a watch at our lips, post a sentinel over our actions; thereby preventing the approach of every unworthy thought or deed, and preserving consciences void of offence towards God and towards man."

CHARGE UPON THE INSTALLATION OF THE OFFICERS OF A LODGE.

"WORSHIPFUL MASTER—

"The Grand Lodge having committed to your care the superintendence and government of the Brethren who are to compose this new Lodge, you cannot be insensible of the obligations which devolve on you as their head; nor of your responsibility for the faithful discharge of the important duties annexed to your appointment.

"The honor, reputation and usefulness of your Lodge, will materially depend on the skill and assiduity with which you manage its concerns; whilst the happiness of its members will be generally promoted, in proportion to the zeal and ability with which you propagate the genuine principles of our Institution.

"For a pattern of imitation, consider the great luminary of nature, which, rising in the *East*, regularly diffuses light and lustre to all within its circle. In like manner it is your province to spread and communicate light and instruction to the Brethren of your Lodge. Forcibly impress upon them the dignity and high importance of Masonry; and seriously admonish them never to disgrace it. Charge them to practice *out* of the Lodge, those duties which they have been taught *in* it; and by amiable, discreet and virtuous conduct, to convince mankind of the goodness of the Institution; so that when a person is said to be a member of it, the world may know that he is one to whom the burthened heart may pour out its sorrows; to whom distress may prefer its suit; whose hand is guided by justice, and his heart is expanded by benevolence. In short, by a diligent observance of the By-Laws of your Lodge, the Constitutions of Masonry, and above all, the Holy

CEREMONY OF INSTALLATION. 59

Scriptures, which are given as a rule and guide to your faith, you will be enabled to acquit yourself with honor and reputation, and lay up a *crown of rejoicing*, which shall continue when time shall be no more.

"BROTHER SENIOR AND JUNIOR WARDENS—

"You are too well acquainted with the principles of Masonry to warrant any distrust that you will be found wanting in the discharge of your respective duties. Suffice it to say, that what you have seen praiseworthy in others, you should carefully imitate; and what in them may have appeared defective, you should in yourselves amend. You should be examples of good order and regularity; for it is only by a due regard to the laws, in your own conduct, that you can expect obedience to them from others. You are assiduously to assist the Master in the discharge of his trust; diffusing light and imparting knowledge to all whom he shall place under your care. In the absence of the Master you will succeed to higher duties; your acquirements must therefore be such, as that the Craft may never suffer for want of proper instruction. From the spirit which you have hitherto evinced, I entertain no doubt that your future conduct will be such as to merit the applause of your Brethren, and the testimony of a good conscience.

"BRETHREN OF ——— LODGE—

"Such is the nature of our Constitution, that as some must of necessity rule and teach, so others must, of course, learn to submit and obey. Humility in both is an essential duty. The officers who are appointed to govern your Lodge, are sufficiently conversant with the rules of propriety, and the laws of the Institution, to avoid exceeding the powers with which they are entrusted; and you are of too generous dispositions to envy their preferment. I therefore trust that you will have but one aim, to please each other, and unite in the grand design of being happy, and communicating happiness.

"Finally, my Brethren, as this association has been formed and perfected in so much unanimity and concord, in which we greatly rejoice, so may it long continue. May you long enjoy every satisfaction and delight, which disinterested friendship can afford. May kindness and Brotherly affection distinguish your conduct as men and as Masons. Within your peaceful walls, may your childrens' children celebrate with joy and gratitude, the annual recurrence of this auspicious solemnity. And may the *tenets of our profession* be transmitted through your Lodge, pure and unimpaired, from generation to generation."

The Grand Marshal then proclaims the new Lodge, in the following manner, viz:

"In the name of the Most Worshipful Grand Lodge of the State of ———, I proclaim this new Lodge, by the name of ——— Lodge, duly constituted."

The Grand Chaplain then makes the concluding prayer, which ends the public ceremonies.

The Grand Procession is then formed in the same order as before, and returns to the hall.

The Grand Master, Deputy Grand Master, and Grand Wardens being seated, all but Master Masons are requested to retire, and the procession continues round the hall, which, upon passing the several Grand Officers, pays them due homage, by the usual congratulation and honors, in the different degrees. During the procession (which passes three times round the Lodge) the following Ode is sung, which concludes the ceremony of Installation.

INSTALLATION ODE.

[Written for the Trestle-Board, by R. W. Br. Thomas Power, Esq., of Boston.]

Tune—"*Indian Philosopher.*"*

When heaven's Great Architect Divine
Raised world on world in kind design,
   Then form on earth was laid;
Fraternal thoughts conferred on man,
By love inspired the social plan,
   And social hearts obeyed.

While wandering on our clouded way,
Compassion shed its kindly ray,
   A guide to lead the blind;
Conducted by a holy light,
With generous love and mystic rite,
   The purest joys we find.

With skill to work, and wise to guide,
No pain shall come, no thought divide,
   Where hearts with heart agree;
Then let us to our altar bring
The dearest offering while we sing,
   United, true and free.

The Lodge is then closed with the usual solemnities in the different degrees, by the Grand Master and his officers.

This is the usual ceremony observed by regular Masons at the Constitution of a new Lodge, which the Grand Master may abridge or extend at pleasure; but the material points are on no account to be omitted. The same ceremony and charges attend every succeeding Installation of new officers.

---

*Arranged as a sacred melody by the name of "*Redeeming Love,*" and "*Ganges.*"

THIRD SECTION.

CEREMONY OBSERVED AT LAYING THE FOUNDATION STONES OF PUBLIC STRUCTURES.

This ceremony is conducted by the Grand Master and his officers, assisted by the members of the Grand Lodge, and such other officers and members of private Lodges as can conveniently attend. The Chief Magistrate, and other civil officers of the place where the building is to be erected, generally attend on the occasion:

At the time appointed, the Grand Lodge is convened in some suitable place, approved by the Grand Master. A band of martial music is provided, and the Brethren appear in the insignia of the Order, and with white gloves and aprons. The Lodge is opened by the Grand Master, and the rules for regulating the procession to and from the place where the ceremony is to be performed, are read by the Grand Secretary. The necessary cautions are then given from the Chair, and the Lodge is adjourned; after which the procession sets out in the following order:

PROCESSION AT LAYING FOUNDATION STONES.

Marshal.

Entered Apprentices;
Fellow-Crafts;
Two Tylers, with drawn Swords;
Tyler of the Oldest Lodge, with a drawn Sword;
Two Stewards of the Oldest Lodge;
Master Masons;
Stewards;
Junior Deacons;
Senior Deacons;
Secretaries;
Treasurers;
Past Wardens;
Junior Wardens;
Senior Wardens;
Mark Masters;
Past Masters;
Royal Arch Masons;
Knights Templars;
Masters;
Music;
Grand Tyler, with a drawn Sword;
Grand Stewards, with White Rods;
A Brother, with a Golden Vessel containing Corn;
Two Brethren, with Silver Vessels, one containing Wine, and the other Oil;
Principal Architect, with Square, Level and Plumb;

Grand Secretary and Treasurer;
Bible, Square and Compass, carried by a Master of a Lodge, supported by two Stewards;
Grand Chaplain;
The Five Orders;
Past Grand Wardens;
Past Deputy Grand Masters;
Past Grand Masters;
Chief Magistrate of the place;
Two large Lights, borne by two Masters of Lodges;
Grand Wardens;
One large Light, borne by a Master of a Lodge;
Deputy Grand Master;
Master of the Oldest Lodge, bearing the Book of Constitutions, on a Velvet Cushion;
Grand Deacons, with Black Rods, on a line seven feet apart;
GRAND MASTER;
Grand Sword Bearer, with a drawn Sword;
Two Stewards, with White Rods.

A triumphal arch is usually erected at the place where the ceremony is to be performed. The procession passes through the arch, and the Brethren repairing to their stands, the Grand Master and his officers take their places on a temporary platform, covered with carpet. The following Hymn may then be sung:

GREAT Architect of earth and heaven,
By time nor space confined,
Enlarge our love to comprehend,
Our BRETHREN, all mankind.

Where'er we are, whate'er we do,
Thy presence let us own;
Thine EYE, all-seeing, marks our deeds
To Thee all thoughts are known.

While nature's works and science's laws,
We labor to reveal,
O! be our duty done to Thee,
With fervency and zeal.

With FAITH our guide, and humble HOPE,
Warm CHARITY and LOVE,
May all at last be raised to share
Thy perfect LIGHT above.

The Grand Master commands silence, and the necessary preparations are made for laying the Stone, on which is engraved the year of Masonry, the name and titles of the Grand Master, &c. &c.

The Stone is raised up, by the means of an engine erected for that purpose, and the Grand Chaplain, or orator, repeats a short prayer. The Grand Treasurer, by the Grand Master's command, places under the Stone various sorts of coin and medals of the present age. Solemn Music is introduced, and the stone let down into its place. The principal architect then presents the working tools to the Grand Master, who applies the *Plumb*, *Square* and *Level* to the Stone, in their proper positions, and pronounces it to be " WELL FORMED, TRUE AND TRUSTY."

The golden and silver vessels are next brought to the table, and delivered, the former to the Deputy Grand Master, and the latter to the Grand Wardens, who successively present them to the Grand Master : and he, according to ancient ceremony, pours the corn, the wine, and the oil, which they contain, on the stone, saying,

"May the all-bounteous Author of Nature bless the inhabitants of this place with all the necessaries, conveniences and comforts of life ; assist in the erection and completion of the building ; protect the workmen against every accident, and long preserve this structure from decay ; and grant to us all, in needed supply, the CORN of *nourishment*, the WINE of *refreshment*, and the OIL *of joy !*"

"*Amen ! so mote it be ! Amen !*"

He then strikes the Stone thrice with the mallet, and the *public* honors of Masonry are given.

The Grand Master then delivers over to the architect the various implements of architecture, entrusting him with the superintendence and direction of the work ; after which, he re-ascends the platform, and an Oration, suitable to the occasion, is delivered. A voluntary collection is made for the workmen, and the sum collected is placed upon the Stone by the Grand Treasurer. The ceremony concludes with the annexed Ode. After which the procession returns to the place whence it set out, and the Lodge is closed.

CONCLUDING ODE.

[Written for the Trestle-Board, by R. W. Br. Thomas Power, Esq., of Boston.]

MUSIC—" *Turin*."

Placed in form the corner stone,—
True and trusty, Brothers own,—
Come and bring, in thought sincere,
Hands to help, and hearts to cheer.

CHORUS.
Come and bring, in thought sincere,
Hands to help, and hearts to cheer.

Marked with love the Master's will—
Kindly proved the work of skill—
Beauteous forms in grace shall rise
'Neath the arch of favoring skies.

CHORUS.
Beauteous forms in grace shall rise
'Neath the arch of favoring skies.

Join we now our off'ring true,
While our homage we renew;
Bear to Him whose praise we sing,
Thanks that from each bosom spring.

CHORUS.
Bear to Him whose praise we sing,
Thanks that from each bosom spring.

When on earth our work is o'er,
Be a dearer life in store,
Each in form, in heart upright,
Taught by Truth's unerring light.

CHORUS.
Each in form, in heart upright,
Taught by Truth's unerring light.

FOURTH SECTION.

CEREMONY OBSERVED AT THE DEDICATION OF MASONIC HALLS.

On the day appointed for the celebration of the ceremony of Dedication, the Grand Master and his officers, accompanied by the members of the Grand Lodge, meet in a convenient room near to the place where the ceremony is to be performed, and the Grand Lodge is opened in ample form, in the first three Degrees of Masonry.

The Master of the Lodge to which the hall to be Dedicated belongs, being present, rises and addresses the Grand Master as follows:

"MOST WORSHIPFUL—

"The Brethren of ——— Lodge, being animated with a desire of promoting the honor and interest of the Craft, have, at great pains and expense, erected a Masonic Hall, for their convenience and accommodation. They are now desirous that the same should be examined by the Most Worshipful Grand Lodge; and if it should meet their approbation, that it should be solemnly dedicated to Masonic purposes, agreeably to ancient form."

The Grand Master then directs the Grand Secretary to read the Order of Procession, which is delivered over to the Grand Marshal; and a General Charge respecting propriety of behavior, is given by the Deputy Grand Master; or the necessary directions are given to the Brethren from the Chair.

A grand procession is then formed in the order laid down in the first section. The whole moves forward to the hall which is to be Dedicated; and upon the arrival of the front of the procession at the door, they halt, open to the right and left, and face inward, whilst the Grand Master, and others in succession, pass through and enter. The Music continues while the procession marches three times round the hall.

The Lodge is placed in the centre. The Grand Master having taken the chair, under a canopy, the Grand Officers take the places of the corresponding officers of the Lodge, and the Masters and Wardens of other Lodges, repair to the places previously prepared for their reception. The three lights, (in a triangular form) and the gold and silver pitchers, with the corn, wine and oil, are placed on the Lodge, at the head of which stands the pedestal, or altar, with the Bible open, and the Square and Compass laid thereon. The Constitution is placed beside it, on a crimson velvet cushion.

The following introductory may then be sung :—

INTRODUCTORY.

[Written for the Trestle-Board, by R. W. Br. Thomas Power, Esq., of Boston.]

Music—"*Effingham.*"

How dear the place where Brothers true
Their holy pledge of Faith renew!

DUETT.
Let notes of love responsive rise,

CHORUS.
From East to West—to farthest skies.

While here sweet hope its presence bears,
No fear indulged, no anxious cares.

DUETT.
Let notes of love responsive rise,

CHORUS.
From East to West—to farthest skies.

May gentle Charity here find,
United friends and Brothers kind.

DUETT.

Let notes of love responsive rise,

CHORUS.

From East to West—to farthest skies.

To Him, our Master throned in Light,
Let every voice, in praise, unite.

DUETT.

Let notes of love responsive rise,

CHORUS.

From East to West—to farthest skies.

After performing the above, and an eulogy on Masonry having been given, the architect addresses the Grand Master as follows :

"MOST WORSHIPFUL—

"Having been entrusted with the superintendence and management of the workmen employed in the construction of this edifice; and having, according to the best of my ability, accomplished the task assigned me ; I now return my thanks for the honor of this appointment, and beg leave to surrender up the implements which were committed to my care when the foundation of this fabric was laid ; humbly hoping, that the exertions which have been made on this occasion, will be crowned with your approbation, and that of the Most Worshipful Grand Lodge."

To which the Grand Master makes the following reply :

"BROTHER ARCHITECT,

"The skill and fidelity displayed in the execution of the trust reposed in you, at the commencement of this undertaking, have secured the entire approbation of the Grand Lodge; and they sincerely pray, that this edifice may continue a lasting monument of the taste, spirit and liberality of its founders."

The following Ode, by the R. W. Br. POWER, may then be sung :—

TUNE—"*Indian Philosopher.*"

When darkness veiled the hopes of man,
Then *Light* with radiant beams began,
   To cheer his clouded way ;
In graceful *Form*, to soothe his woes,
Then *Beauty* to his vision rose,
   In bright and gentle ray.

Immortal *order* stood confessed,
From farthest *East* to distant *West*,
   In columns just and true ;
The faithful *Plumb* and *Level* there,
Uniting with the mystic *Square*,
   The temple brought to view.

DEDICATION OF MASONIC HALLS.

Descending then from Heaven Most High,
Came *Charity* with tearful eye,
    To dwell with feeble man;
Hope whispered peace in brighter skies
On which a trusting *Faith* relies,
    And earth's best joys began.

Abroad was seen the boon of Heaven,
Fraternal Love was kindly given,
    And touched each kindred heart;
The sons of Light with transport then,
In kindness to their fellow-men,
    Unveiled the *Mystic Art*.

Let grateful pæans loudly rise,
O'er earth's domains, to azure skies,
    As time shall onward move;
A Brother's joy and wo shall be,
Undying bonds to mark *the free*,
    To wake a Brother's love.

The Deputy Grand Master then rises and says:

"Most Worshipful—

"The hall in which we are now assembled, and the plan upon which it has been constructed, having met with your approbation, it is the desire of the Fraternity that it should be now Dedicated, according to ancient form and usage."

Whereupon the Grand Master requests all to retire but such as are Master Masons. A procession is then formed in the following order, viz.

    Grand Sword Bearer;
    A Past Master, with a Light;
A Past Master, with Bible, Square and Compass, on a Velvet Cushion;
    Two Past Masters, each with a Light;
    Grand Secretary and Treasurer, with Emblems;
    Grand Junior Warden, with Pitcher of Corn;
    Grand Senior Warden, with Pitcher of Wine;
    Deputy Grand Master, with Pitcher of Oil;
    Grand Master;
    Two Stewards, with Rods.

All the other Brethren keep their places, and assist in performing the following Ode, which continues during the procession, excepting only at the intervals of Dedication.

[Written for the Trestle-Board, by R. W. Br. Thomas Power, Esq., of Boston.]

Music—"*Sterling.*"

All honors to our Master pay,
  Who bade our holy temple rise;
While here we journey on our way,
  Our thanks shall reach to farthest skies.
    (Dedication to FREEMASONRY.)

We hail our holy Patron's name,
  Whose bright example guides us still;
His highest honors we proclaim,
  While grateful thanks our temple fill.
    (Dedication to VIRTUE.)

While thus we seek, in pure desire,
  Immortal bliss in realms above,
Our hearts shall kindle at the fire
  Whose light is Universal Love.
    (Dedication to UNIVERSAL BENEVOLENCE.)

The Lodge is uncovered, and the first procession being made round it, the Grand Master having reached the East, the Grand Junior Warden presents the pitcher of corn to the Grand Master, who, striking thrice with his mallet, pours it out upon the Lodge, at the same time pronouncing, "In the name of the great Jehovah, to whom be all honor and glory, I do solemnly dedicate this hall to FREEMASONRY." *The grand honors are given.*

The second procession is then made round the Lodge, and the Grand Senior Warden presents the pitcher of wine to the Grand Master, who sprinkles it upon the Lodge, at the same time saying, "In the name of holy Saint John, I do solemnly dedicate this hall to VIRTUE." *The grand honors are twice repeated.*

The third procession is then made round the Lodge, and the Deputy Grand Master presents the pitcher of oil to the Grand Master, who sprinkling it upon the Lodge, says, "In the name of the whole Fraternity, I do solemnly dedicate this hall to UNIVERSAL BENEVOLENCE." *The Grand honors are thrice repeated.*

A solemn invocation is made to Heaven, by the Grand Chaplain, and an anthem sung; after which the Lodge is covered, and the Grand Master retires to his chair. An oration is then delivered by some Brother appointed for the purpose, and the ceremonies conclude with music. The Grand Lodge is again formed in procession, as at first, and returns to the room whence it was opened, and is closed in ample form.

FIFTH SECTION.

THE CEREMONY OBSERVED AT FUNERALS, ACCORDING TO THE ANCIENT CUSTOM; WITH TWO SERVICES, EITHER OF WHICH MAY BE USED ON THE OCCASION.

No Mason can be interred with the formalities of the Order unless he has been advanced to the Third Degree of Masonry. Fellow-Crafts, or Apprentices, are not entitled to funeral obsequies, nor to attend the Masonic Processions on such occasions.

All the Brethren who walk in procession, should observe, as much as possible, a uniformity in their dress. Black clothes, with white gloves and aprons, are most suitable.

FORM OF SERVICE,

Drawn up by Rev. ALBERT CASE, *of South Carolina, and adopted by the National Masonic Convention, at Baltimore, May,* 1843.

The Brethren having assembled, the presiding Officer opens the Lodge in the Third Degree in Masonry.

After the object of the meeting has been stated, the Chaplain, or Master, will begin the service as follows:—

SERVICE IN THE LODGE ROOM.

1. If a man die, shall he live again?

Response—The dust shall return to the earth as it was, and the spirit shall return to God who gave it.

II. When he dieth, shall he carry any thing away with him?

Response—He brought nothing into this world, and it is certain he can carry nothing out.

III. The Lord gave, and the Lord hath taken away; blessed be the name of the Lord.

Response—God is our God forever. He will be our guide and support through the dark valley of the shadow of death.

Our Brother has been called from labor in the terrestrial Lodge, and gone, we trust, to partake of the divine refreshments on high.

Let us meditate on the virtues of his character—the benevolent spirit he manifested—the offerings he made upon the altar of charity, whereby the needy were supported—the distressed comforted—the widow's woes assuaged, and the lone orphan's tears dried up.

Let us see in the holy precepts of religion and in the teachings of our Institution, those principles which influenced him to adore his Maker, and to love his fellow-man, and which taught him how to live and how to die.

And since he has gone, in obedience to Heaven's mandate, may the recollection of his honor and virtue be cherished in our hearts, and have a salutary influence in our lives.

And now, beloved Brother, farewell, farewell, till we meet thee with a lasting embrace in that Grand Lodge, where the Grand Master Supreme, forever presides, forever reigns!

THE HONORS ARE THEN GIVEN, AND THE FOLLOWING PRAYER PRONOUNCED.

Almighty God—infinite in wisdom, mercy and goodness, extend to us the riches of thy everlasting favor, make us grateful for present benefits, and crown us with immortal life and honor. And to thy name shall be glory forever.—*Amen!*

The procession is then formed and proceeds to the place of interment. While assembling around the grave, sacred music may be performed.

ORDER OF PROCESSION AT A FUNERAL.

Tyler, with a Drawn Sword;
Stewards, with White Rods;
Musicians, (if they are Masons, otherwise they follow the Tyler;)
Master Masons;
Senior and Junior Deacons;
Secretary and Treasurer;
Senior and Junior Wardens;
Past Masters;
The Holy Writings, on a Cushion covered with Black Cloth, carried by the oldest Member of the Lodge;
The Master;
Clergy;

The		Body,
with the insignia		placed thereon,
and two		Swords crossed;
Pall Bearers.		Pall Bearers.

The officers take their position at the head of the grave, and the following service is performed by the Chaplain or Master:

FUNERAL SERVICE AT THE GRAVE.

My Brethren,

We are now assembled around the final resting place of these mortal remains, and are about closing the last solemn duties of respect we owe to our departed friend and Brother. A few reflections, therefore, applicable to the solemnities of this occssion, and salutary and impressive to the living, may be, with great propriety, offered on this sacred spot—a spot where departed friendship yet lingers, and steals in melancholy, yet pleasing reminiscence on the heart.

We are born to die. We follow our friends to the brink of the grave, and standing on the shore of a vast ocean, we gaze with exquisite anxiety till the last dreadful struggle is over, and see them sink in the fathomless abyss. We feel our own feet slide from the precarious bank on which we stand, and but a few suns more, and we shall be whelmed mid death's awful waves.

The younger are crowding the next older off the stage of action, as though each were anxious to exhibit his part in the strange and ever changeful drama of human life. Not a solitary individual re-enters the world's theatre. All take their exit, and are known beneath the sun no more forever.

We are now in the solemn grave-yard, and here learn the only language of the tomb—the epitaph declaring *they once lived*.

Lettered stones and monuments are more instructive than the once living thousands, whose memories they preserve from oblivion.

All, except these, is speechless as the chambers of eternal silence. No lingering spirits hover around their mouldering relics, whispering any intelligence of their present existence.

The eternal country, for which they embarked, returns us no intelligence of their safe arrival. Speechless is the gentle breeze that fans their verdant covering.

The statesman, hero, philosopher, theologian, whose eloquence or arms have shaken empires—who have united the language of earth and heaven, or plucked proud laurels from fields of war, are resting in silence. Their hearts, that once beat high with hopes of life and glory, are unaffected with the interests of earth, and susceptible of nought but the feelings that appertain to another world.

Not only these are gone, but even the youth, whose cheeks are mantled with sunny smiles, and whose eye sparkles in all the brilliancy of health, must soon become an inanimate lump of clay. Those lips, that now echo the sentiments of inexperience, must be silent, and the heart that now palpitates and rejoices at the sound of pleasure, must be stilled in the cold and cheerless mansions of the dead. Another generation will arise to occupy our places and stations in life.

The sun will rise and set, the earth revolve,—strangers will tread upon our sepulchres, without knowing that we ever existed. A few surviving relatives may remember us and mourn, but these few will soon follow to the land of silence. No one here, will concern himself with our past joys or sorrows, while we shall be conversant with the amazing realities of another world.

Under these feelings and impressions we are now about to commit the body of our departed friend to the silent grave. And under a full and solemn conviction of the nothingness of all earthly and perishable objects, we here renewedly, as Masons, pledge to each other our fraternal love; and may we so improve this dispensation of Divine Providence, and so live, that when these feeble frames shall slumber beneath the cold clods of the valley, the needy and distressed, the widow and the orphan may point with regret to our sleeping ashes, and each exclaim—there lie the men whose compassion soothed my woes; whose maxims tranquillized my perturbed spirits, and whose bounty relieved my pressing necessity.

INVOCATIONS.

I. May we be true and faithful—live and die in love; for the memory of the just is blessed.

Response—So mote it be.

II. The Lord bless us, and keep us—the Lord make his face to shine upon us, and be gracious unto us—the Lord lift upon us the light of his countenance and give us peace.

Response—So mote it be.

All—Glory be to God in the highest, on earth, peace, good will toward men.

PRAYER.

Almighty and most merciful Father, we adore thee as the God of time and of eternity. Of both worlds, thou art the incomprehensible and amazing Lord; ruling the destinies of all; from the highest angel in heaven through every grade of creatures even down to the sparrow's fall—from the grandeur of rolling worlds down to the numbering of the hairs of our heads.

Under a government so vast and minute, we every where see thy ever working hand. We see it in giving us being, and in calling us hence to be here no more.

As it has pleased thee to take from the light of our abode, one dear to our hearts, we beseech thee to bless and sanctify to us this dispensation of thy Providence. Inspire our hearts with wisdom from on high, that we may glorify thee in all our ways. May we realize that thine All-seeing Eye is upon us, and be influenced by the spirit of truth and love to perfect obedience,—that we may enjoy the divine approbation here below. And when our toils on earth shall have ceased, may we be raised to the enjoyment of fadeless light and immortal life in that kingdom, where faith and hope shall end—and love and joy prevail through eternal ages.

And thine, O righteous Father, shall be the glory forever.—*Amen*.

BRETHREN—

We have taken a solemn and impressive survey of human life, in all its blended lights and shades, and learned that all on earth is change. We have seen that as the lightning writes its fiery path on the dark cloud and expires, so the race of men, walking amidst the surrounding shades of mortality, glitter a moment through the darksome gloom, then vanishes from our sight forever.

They rest in the stilly shades. There the worm shall cover us, and darkness and silence reign around our melancholy abode.

But, is this the end of man, and the expiring hope of faithful Masons? No; blessed be God! We pause not at our first or second step, but, true to our principles, we look forward for greater light! As the embers of mortal life are feebly glimmering in the socket of existence, our religion removes the dark shroud, draws aside the sable curtains of the tomb, and bids hope and joy to rouse up, sustain, and cheer the departing spirit. She points beyond the silent tomb, to the breaking light of a resurrection morn, and bids us turn an eye of faith and confidence on the opening scenes of eternity.

She teaches us to advance boldly onward, and ask more light, till at the Grand Master's Word, we shall be *raised* to that blissful LODGE which no time can remove. There light, unmingled with darkness, shall reign unbroken and perpetual. There, under the sun-beam smiles of immutable LOVE, and beneath the benignant bend of the ALL-SEEING EYE, we, as faithful Masons, cherish the fond and immortal hope, that we shall meet again; meet, to part no more.

Unto the grave we now resign the body of our departed Brother.

(Pass round the grave and drop the evergreen, during which time the following Dirge may be sung.)

[Written for the Trestle-Board, by R. W. Br. Thomas Power, Esq., of Boston.]

MUSIC—"*Canterbury.*"

WHAT sounds of grief, in sadness, tell
   A Brother's earthly doom—
No more in life's fair scenes to dwell —
   A tenant of the tomb!

No more the friendly hand now pressed,
   No gently wispered word,
He finds a long, unbroken rest
   Where rules his Heavenly Lord.

All earthly joys and sorrows o'er,
   Each changing hope or fear,
He sees the light of that fair shore
   Without a sigh or tear.

Then bring to him, whose holy care
   That better temple forms,
Our wish that all may gather there,
   Beyond life's coming storms.

Friend of our hearts, there rest in peace. Raised by the Grand Master's Word, mayest thou share the blessing of immortal life, and unfading glory.

The procession then returns to the Lodge in inverse order. When the necessary duties are performed, and the Lodge is closed.

FUNERAL SERVICE.

[By Br. WILLIAM PRESTON. Retained by vote of the Convention.]

The Brethren being assembled at the Lodge room (or some other convenient place) the presiding Master opens the Lodge, in the Third Degree, with the usual forms; and having stated the purpose of the meeting, the service begins:

Master. "What man is he that liveth, and shall not see death? Shall he deliver his soul from the hand of the grave?"

Response. "Man walketh in a vain shadow; he heapeth up riches, and cannot tell who shall gather them."

Master. "When he dieth, he shall carry nothing away; his glory shall not descend after him."

Response. "Naked he came into the world, and naked he must return."

Master. "The Lord gave, and the Lord hath taken away; blessed be the name of the Lord!"

The grand honors are then given, and certain forms used, which cannot be here explained.

The Master then, taking the SACRED ROLL in his hand, says,

"Let us die the death of the righteous, and let our last end be like his!"

The Brethren answer,

"God is our God for ever and ever; he will be our guide even unto death!"

The Master then records the name and age of the deceased upon the roll, and says,

"Almighty Father! Into thy hands we commend the soul of our loving Brother."

The Brethren answer three times (giving the grand honors each time.)

"The will of God is accomplished! So be it."

The Master then deposits the roll in the archives, and repeats the following prayer:

"Most glorious God! Author of all good, and giver of all mercy! Pour down thy blessings upon us, and strengthen our solemn engagements with the ties of sincere affection! May the present instance of mortality remind us of our approaching fate, and draw our attention toward thee, the only refuge in time of need! That when the awful moment shall arrive, that we are about to quit this transitory scene, the enlivening prospect of thy mercy may dispel the gloom of death; and after our departure hence in peace and in thy favor, we may be received into thine everlasting kingdom, to enjoy, in union with the souls of our departed friends, the just reward of a pious and virtuous life. *Amen.*"

A procession is then formed, which moves to the house of the deceased, and from thence to the place of interment. The different Lodges rank according to seniority, excepting that the Lodge, of which the deceased was a member, walks nearest the corpse. Each Lodge forms one division, and the following order is observed:

ORDER OF PROCESSION AT A FUNERAL.

Tyler, with a Drawn Sword;
Stewards, with White Rods;
Musicians, (if they are Masons, otherwise they follow the Tyler;)
Master Masons;
Senior and Junior Deacons;
Secretary and Treasurer;

FUNERAL CEREMONIES.

Senior and Junior Wardens;
Past Masters;
The Holy Writings, on a Cushion covered with Black Cloth, carried by the Oldest Member of the Lodge;
The Master;
Clergy;

The	Body,
with the insignia	placed thereon,
and two	Swords crossed;
Pall Bearers.	Pall Bearers.

The Brethren are not to desert their ranks, or change places, but keep in their different departments. When the procession arrives at the Church yard, the members of the Lodge form a circle round the grave, and the clergyman and officers of the acting Lodge take their station at the head of the grave, and the mourners at the foot, the service is resumed, and the following exhortation given:

"Here we view a striking instance of the uncertainty of life, and the vanity of all human pursuits. The last offices paid to the dead are only useful as lectures to the living; from them we are to derive instruction, and consider every solemnity of this kind as a summons to prepare for our approaching dissolution.

"Notwithstanding the various mementos of mortality with which we daily meet, notwithstanding death has established his empire over all the works of nature, yet through some unaccountable infatuation, we forget that we are born to die. We go on from one design to another, add hope to hope, and lay out plans for the employment of many years, till we are suddenly alarmed with the approach of death, when we least expect him, and at an hour which we probably conclude to be the meridian of our existence.

"What are all the externals of majesty, the pride of wealth, or charms of beauty, when nature has paid her just debts? Fix your eyes on the last scene, and view life stript of her ornaments, and exposed in her natural meanness; you will then be convinced of the futility of those empty delusions. In the grave, all fallacies are detected, all ranks are levelled, and all distinctions are done away.

"While we drop the sympathetic tear over the grave of our deceased friend, let charity incline us to throw a veil over his foibles, whatever they may have been, and not withhold from his memory the praise that his virtues may have claimed. Suffer the apologies of human nature to plead in his behalf. Perfection on earth has never been attained; the wisest, as well as the best of men, have erred.

"Let the present example excite our most serious thoughts, and strengthen our resolutions of amendment. As life is uncertain, and all earthly pursuits are vain, let us no longer postpone the important concern of preparing for eternity; but embrace the happy moment, while time and opportunity offer, to provide against the great change, when all the pleasures of this world shall cease to delight, and the reflections of a virtuous life yield the only comfort and consolation. Thus our expectations will not be frustrated, nor we hurried unprepared into the presence of an all-wise and powerful Judge, to whom the secrets of all hearts are known.

"Let us, while in this state of existence, support with propriety the character of our profession, advert to the nature of our solemn ties, and pursue with assiduity the sacred tenets of our Order. Then, with becoming reverence, let us supplicate the Divine Grace, to ensure the favor of that eternal Being, whose goodness and power know no bound; that when the awful moment arrives, be it soon or late, we may be enabled to prosecute our journey, without dread or apprehension, to that far distant country whence no traveller returns."

The following invocations are then made by the Master:

Master. "May we be true and faithful; and may we live and die in love!"

Answer. "So mote it be."

Master. "May we profess what is good, and always act agreeably to our profession.

Answer. "So mote it be."

Master. May the Lord bless us, and prosper us; and may all our good intentions be crowned with success!"

Answer. "So mote it be."

Master. "Glory be to God on high! On earth peace! Good will towards men!"

Answer. "So mote it be, now, from henceforth, and for evermore."

The Brethren then move in procession round the place of interment, and severally drop a sprig of evergreen* into the grave, accompanied with the usual honors.

The Master then concludes the ceremony at the grave in the following words:

"From time immemorial it has been a custom among the Fraternity of Free and Accepted Masons, at the request of a Brother, to accompany his corpse to the place of interment, and there to deposit his remains with the usual formalities.

"In conformity to this usage, and at the special request of our deceased Brother, whose memory we revere, and whose loss we now deplore, we have assembled in the character of Masons, to resign his body to the earth whence it came, and to offer up to his memory, before the world, the last tribute of our affection, thereby demonstrating the sincerity of our past esteem, and our steady attachment to the principles of the Order.

---

*This is an emblem of our faith in the immortality of the soul, and reminds us that we have an immortal part within us, which shall survive the grave.

"The Great Creator having been pleased, out of his mercy, to remove our Brother from the cares and troubles of a transitory existence, to a state of eternal duration, and thereby to weaken the chain by which we are united, man to man ; may we, who survive him, anticipate our approaching fate, and be more strongly cemented in the ties of union and friendship ; that, during the short space allotted to our present existence, we may wisely and usefully employ our time ; and, in the reciprocal intercourse of kind and friendly acts, mutually promote the welfare and happiness of each other.

"Unto the grave we resign the body of our deceased friend, there to remain until the general resurrection ; in favorable expectation that his immortal soul may then partake of joys which have been prepared for the righteous from the beginning of the world. And may Almighty God, of his infinite goodness, at the grand tribunal of unbiassed justice, extend his mercy towards him, and all of us, and crown our hope with everlasting bliss in the expanded realms of a boundless eternity! This we beg, for the honor of His name ; to whom be glory, now and forever. *Amen.*"

Thus the service ends, and the procession returns in form to the place whence it set out, where the necessary duties are complied with, and the business of Masonry is renewed. The insignia and ornaments of the deceased, if an officer of a Lodge, are returned to the Master, with the usual ceremonies, after which the charges for regulating the conduct of the Brethren are rehearsed, and the Lodge is closed in the Third Degree.

NOTES.

If a past or present Grand Master should join the procession of a private lodge, or Deputy Grand Master, or a Grand Warden, a proper attention is to be paid to them. They take place after the Master of the Lodge. Two deacons, with black rods, are appointed by the Master to attend a Grand Warden ; and when the Grand Master is present, or Deputy Grand Master, the Book of Constitutions is borne before him, a Sword Bearer follows him, and the Deacons, with black rods, are placed on his right and left, at an angular distance of seven feet.

Marshals are to walk, or ride, on the left of the procession.

On entering public buildings, the Bible, Square and Compass, Book of Constitutions, &c. are placed before the Grand Master. The Grand Marshals and Grand Deacons shall keep near him.

CHAPTER X.

ADDRESSES AND PRAYERS FOR OCCASIONAL USE.
ADDRESSES.

ADDRESS TO A GRAND MASTER AT HIS INSTALLATION.

I AM desired, Most Worshipful, to install you into your high office, as Grand Master of Masons.

Give me leave to invest you with this BADGE of your office. This will silently admonish you always to do justice to the cause of Masonry; to consult, as the exalted rank you now hold demands of you, its real interests. It will instruct you to infuse into the many Lodges, of which you are now the head, the true spirit of our Order. It will direct you to make wise regulations for the good government of the Fraternity; to give due commendation to the worthy members of it; and to rebuke those who act contrary to its laws.

I next deliver to you the EMBLEM OF THAT POWER with which you are now invested. Always make use of it for the good of our benevolent Institution.

To you are committed, also, those SACRED WRITINGS in which are to be found the sublime parts of our ancient mystery. In them are, likewise, most strongly inculcated the social and moral duties, without which no man can be a Mason. You will direct your Lodges to read, study, and obey them.

Receive *these* TOOLS *of* OPERATIVE MASONRY, which are to each of us the most expressive symbols. These will assist you, Most Worshipful, to reduce all matter into proper form; to bring to due subjection irregular passions, and to circumscribe them by harmony, order, and duty.

And lastly, I present to you the BOOK OF CONSTITUTIONS, in which are contained the *rules* and *orders* made for the good government of the Society; and the *Charges*, which show its nature, its wisdom, and its utility. With this book, Most Worshipful, you will direct your Lodges to make themselves well acquainted—a work, in all its parts, worthy the attention of men the most enlightened and judicious.

You are now, Most Worshipful, at the head of an Order which is calculated to unite men by true friendship; to extend benevolence, and to promote virtue. And, give me leave to say, that the honor with which you are invested is not unworthy of a man of the highest rank, or most distinguished abilities. Permit me, also, to remind you, that your faithful attention to the duties of your office, and acceptable discharge of them, will render you of great benefit to one of the most liberal Institutions upon earth.

May you do honor to your exalted station; and long enjoy the highest respect and best wishes of all the Fraternity.

ADDRESS AT INITIATION OF A CLERGYMAN.

You, Brother, are a preacher of that religion, which inculcates universal benevolence and unbounded charity. You will, therefore, be fond of the order, and zealous for the interests of FREEMASONRY, which, in the strongest manner, inculcates the same charity and benevolence, and which, like that religion, encourages every moral and social virtue; which introduces peace and good will among mankind. So that whoever is warmed with the spirit of Christianity, must esteem, must love FREEMASONRY.

Here, virtue, the grand object in view, luminous as the meridian sun, shines refulgent on the mind; enlivens the heart, and warms with sympathy and affection.

Though every man, who carefully listens to the dictates of reason, may arrive at a clear persuasion of the beauty and necessity of virtue, both private and public, yet it is a full recommendation of a society, to have these pursuits continually in view, as the sole object of their association: and these are the laudable bonds which unite us in one indissoluble Fraternity.

ADDRESS AT INITIATION OF A FOREIGNER.

You, Brother, the native and subject of another nation, by entering into our Order, have connected yourself, by sacred and affectionate ties, with thousands of Masons in this and other countries. Ever recollect that the Order you have entered into, bids you always to look upon the world as ONE GREAT REPUBLIC, of which every nation is a family, and every particular person a child. When, therefore, you return and settle in your own country, take care that the progress of friendship be not confined to the narrow circle of national connections, or particular religions; but let it be *universal*, and extend to every branch of the human race. At the same time remember that, besides the common ties of humanity, you have at this time entered into obligations, which engage you to kind and friendly actions to your Brother Masons, of whatever station, country, or religion.

ADDRESS AT INITIATION OF A SOLDIER.

OUR institution breathes a spirit of general philanthropy. Its benefits, considered in a social view, are extensive. It unites all mankind. It in every nation opens an asylum to virtue in distress, and grants hospitality to the necessitous and unfortunate. The sublime principles of universal goodness and love to all mankind, which are essential to it, cannot be lost in national distinctions, prejudices, and animosities. The rage of contest it has abated, and substituted in its stead the milder emotions of humanity. It has even taught the pride of victory to give way to the dictates of an honorable connection.

Should your country demand your services in foreign wars, and captivity should be your portion, may you find affectionate Brethren where others would only find enemies.

In whatever nation you travel, when you meet a Mason, you will find a Brother and a friend, who will do all in his power to serve you; and who will relieve you, should you be poor or in distress, to the utmost of his ability, and with ready cheerfulness.

PRAYERS.

PRAYER AT INITIATION.

Thou Supreme! Author of peace and lover of concord—bless us in the exercise of those kind and social affections thou hast given us. May we cherish and display them as our honor and our joy. May this our friend, who is now to become our Brother, devote his life to thy service, and consider aright the true principles of his engagements. May he be endowed with Wisdom to direct him in all his ways; Strength to support him in all his difficulties; and Beauty to adorn his moral conduct. And may we jointly and individually walk within compass, and square our actions by the dictates of conscience and virtue, and the example of the wise and good. Amen.

ANOTHER.

Grand Architect! Behold us aspiring towards thee. Thy works fill us with rapture. Heaven's gates stand open to welcome thy sons to glory!

Behold our friend, and soon to be our Brother! entering upon the threshold, which is before this apartment in thy works. May love burst the silence around him, and salute him welcome at the first step. May joy triumph in his heart, and friendship guide him as he ascends. May his countenance be cheered by the light, and confidence increase as he passes on. May he behold the emblems of his labor, and his heart reply in ready obedience. May the cheerfulness inspired by the dawning light, attend him through the day: And when a long day is complete, may he find his lot with the faithful, in the immortal glory of the Temple, which is pure with the light of God, and eternal in the Heavens!

ANOTHER.

O THOU, whose Temple we are! On the mountain of thy truth, let our sublime edifice display its glory. Let the eye of the Master meet the Son of Light as he enters. Let the greater lights, by the help of the less, illuminate the whole scene of his duty and of his pleasure. Behold us with thy brightness, at this hour, leading a young son into thy Temple. Like the Temple, let him be beauteous without, and all glorious within. Let his soul be capacious as thy truth, and his affections pure as the serene heavens, when the silent Moon gives her light. Let him obey as the Sun, who labors until perfect day, with increasing strength; and let all the purposes of his heart be as the Stars which tell of worlds unknown, and are notices of boundless benevolence. Let him move like the heavenly orbs in harmony; and should he stretch across the Universe, may he disturb no soul in his course. Within this Temple may he be sacred as the altar, sweet as the incense, and pure as the most holy place. Among thy ministering servants, may he be ready as an angel of GOD, and faithful as a beloved Son. And when his service is finished, may his memory be celebrated by love, on the durable monuments of eternity; and his reward, in the silent solemn joy of heaven, be sure from the hand of GOD, the Grand Master of us all.

PRAYER AT OPENING GRAND LODGE.

[From the Archives of the Grand Lodge of Massachusetts.]

O MOST glorious and eternal God, the infinitely wise Architect of the Universe; we, thy servants, assembled in solemn Grand Lodge, would extol thy power and wisdom.

Thou saidst, Let there be light, and there was light. The heavens opened and declared thy glory; and the firmament spangled with thy handy work. The sun, who rules the day, gave light to the moon, who rules the night surrounded with the stars. So that there is one glory of the sun, another glory of the moon, and one star differs from another star in glory; and all, by most wondrous signs and tokens, without voice, sound, or language, solemnly proclaim thy divine mysteries.

We adore thee for our creation; for the breath of life; for the light of reason and conscience; and for all the noble and useful faculties of our souls; which give us so exalted a rank in the order of being. Enable us to live answerably to our exalted privileges and happy destination.

We beseech thee to give us, thy servants, at this, and at all times, wisdom in all our doings; strength of mind in our difficulties; and the beauty of harmony in all our communications with one another.

Grant, that thy servant, who has been solemnly invested with authority and rule, over these Lodges, may be endued with knowledge and wisdom; and may we, and all our Brethren under his jurisdiction, understand, learn, and keep all the statutes and commandments of the LORD, pure and undefiled. May brotherly love and charity always abound among us. And when we have finished our work here below, let our transition be from this earthly tabernacle to the heavenly temple above; there, among thy jewels, may we appear in thy glory forever and ever.

Bless and prosper, we pray thee, every branch and member of this Fraternity, throughout the habitable earth. May thy kingdom of peace, love, and harmony come. May thy will be done on earth, as it is in heaven, and the whole world be filled with thy glory. AMEN.

PRAYER AT CONSTITUTING A LODGE.
[By Rev. Br. Dr. JOHN WATKINS.]

GREAT, Adorable and Supreme Being! We praise thee for all thy mercies, and especially for giving us desires to enjoy, and powers of enjoying, the delights of society. The affections which thou hast implanted in us, and which we cannot destroy without violence to our nature, are among the chief blessings which thy benign wisdom hath bestowed upon us: help us duly to improve all our powers to the promotion of thy glory in the world, and the good of our fellow-creatures.

May we be active under thy divine light, and dwell in thy truth.

Extend thy favor to us who are now entering into a Fraternal compact under peculiar obligations. Enable us to be faithful to thee, faithful in our callings in life, faithful Masons in all the duties of the Craft, and faithful to each other as members of this society. Take us under the shadow of thy protection; and to thy service and glory may we consecrate our hearts. May we always put *faith* in thee, have *hope* in salvation, and be in *charity* with all mankind! AMEN.

CHAPTER XI.

FORMS TO BE USED FOR VARIOUS MASONIC PURPOSES.

FORM OF PETITION FOR DISPENSATION FOR NEW LODGE.

To the Most Worshipful Grand Master of the Grand Lodge of Ancient Free and Accepted Masons of the State of ———.

We, the undersigned, being Master Masons of good standing, and having the prosperity of the Craft at heart, are anxious o exert our best endeavors to promote and diffuse the genuine principles of Freemasonry; and, for the convenience of our respective dwellings and other good reasons, we are desirous of forming a new Lodge, to be named ———. We, therefore, with the approbation of the District Deputy Grand Master and the Lodge nearest our residence, respectfully pray for a Dispensation, empowering us to meet as a regular Lodge, at ———, on the ——— of every month, and there to discharge the duties of Ancient York Masonry, in a constitutional manner, according to the forms of the Order and the laws of the Grand Lodge. And we have nominated and do recommend Brother A. B., to be the first Master, Brother C. D., to be the first Senior Warden, and Brother E. F., to be the first Junior Warden of the said Lodge. The prayer of this petition being granted, we promise strict obedience to the commands of the Grand Master, and the laws and regulations of the Grand Lodge.

FORM OF A DISPENSATION FOR A NEW LODGE.

To all whom it may concern:

Greeting.

WHEREAS, a Petition has been presented to me by sundry Brethren, to wit: Brothers A., B., and C., residing in the town of ———, and State of ———, praying to be congregated into a regular Lodge, and promising to render obedience to the ancient usages and landmarks of the Fraternity, and the laws of the Grand Lodge: And whereas, said Petitioners have been recommended to me as MASTER MASONS, in good standing, by the Master, Wardens, and other members of ——— Lodge, under our jurisdiction,

Therefore, I, ——— ———, Grand Master of the M. W. Grand Lodge of the State of ———, reposing full confidence in the recommendation aforesaid, and in the Masonic integrity and ability of the petitioners, do, by virtue of the authority in me vested, hereby grant this DISPENSATION, empowering and authorizing our trusty and well-beloved Brethren aforesaid, to form and open a LODGE, after the manner of *Ancient Free and Accepted Masons*, and therein to admit and make FREEMASONS, *according to the ancient custom, and not otherwise.*

This dispensation is to continue in full force for the term of ———, [or until the next annual communication of our Grand Lodge aforesaid,] unless sooner revoked by me. And I do hereby appoint Br. A. B., to be the first Master, Br. C. D., to be the first Senior Warden, and Br. E. F., to be the first Junior Warden, of the said new LODGE. And it shall be their duty, and they are hereby required, to return this DISPENSATION, with a correct transcript of all PROCEEDINGS had under the authority of the same, together with an attested copy of their BY-LAWS, to our Grand Lodge aforesaid, at the expiration of the time herein specified,—for examination, and such further action in the premises, as shall then be deemed wise and proper.

Given under our hand, and the seal of our Grand Lodge aforesaid, at ———, this —— day of ———, A. L. 58—, A. D. 18—.

——— ———, *Grand Master.*

Attest,

——— ———, *Grand Secretary.*

FORM OF A CHARTER, OR WARRANT, FOR A NEW LODGE.

𝔗o all the 𝔉raternity to whom these 𝔓resents shall come:
The GRAND LODGE *of the Most Ancient and Honorable Society of Free and Accepted* MASONS *for the* ——— *of* ———, *sends Greeting:*

[SEAL.]

———, G. M.
———, D. G. M.

WHEREAS a petition has been presented to us by [*Here insert the names of the Petitioners*] all Ancient, Free, and Accepted Masons, praying that they, with such others, as shall hereafter join them, may be erected and constituted into a regular Lodge of Free and Accepted Masons—which Petition appearing to us as tending to the advancement of Masonry and the good of the Craft:

𝔎now ye, therefore, That We, the Grand Lodge aforesaid, reposing special trust and confidence in the prudence and fidelity of our beloved Brethren above named, have constituted and appointed, and by these Presents, do constitute and appoint them, the said A., B., I., F., &c. a regular Lodge of Free and Accepted Masons, under the Title and Designation of ——— Lodge, No. —, hereby giving and granting unto them and their successors, full power and authority to convene as Masons, within the Town of ———, in the County of ———, and State of ———, aforesaid—to receive and enter Apprentices, pass Fellow-Crafts, and raise Master Masons, upon the payment of such moderate compensations for the same, as may be determined by the said Lodge: Also to make choice of a Master, Wardens, and other Office Bearers, annually, or otherwise, as they shall see cause; to receive and collect Funds for the relief of poor and distressed Brethren, their Widows or Children, and in general to transact all matters relating to Masonry, which may to them appear to be for the good of the Craft, according to the ancient usages and customs of Masons.

And we do hereby require the said constituted Brethren, to attend the Grand Lodge at its regular Communications, and other Meetings, by their Master and Wardens, or by Proxies regularly appointed; also to keep a fair and regular Record of all their proceedings, and to lay them before the Grand Lodge when required.

And we do enjoin upon our Brethren of the said Lodge, that they be punctual in the payment of such sums as may be assessed for the support of the Grand Lodge—that they behave themselves respectfully and obediently to their superiors in office, and in all other respects conduct themselves as good Masons.

And we do hereby declare the precedence of the said Lodge, in the Grand Lodge and elsewhere, to commence from ———.

𝕴𝖓 𝕿𝖊𝖘𝖙𝖎𝖒𝖔𝖓𝖞 𝖜𝖍𝖊𝖗𝖊𝖔𝖋 We, the Grand Master and Grand Wardens, by virtue of the power and authority to us committed, have hereunto set our hands, and caused the seal of the Grand Lodge to be affixed, at ———, this ——— day of ———, Anno Domini ———, and of Masonry ———.

          I. T., *Senior Grand Warden.*
          I. L., *Junior Grand Warden.*

By Order of the Grand Lodge,
   Attest,   D. O., *Grand Secretary.*

FORM OF POWER FOR CONSTITUTING A LODGE.

From the East of the Most Worshipful Grand Lodge of ———.

TO ALL WHOM IT MAY CONCERN:

But more especially to Brothers A. B., Worshipful Master elect; C. D., Senior Warden elect; and E. F., Junior Warden elect, and the rest of the Brethren, who have been empowered by warrant of Constitution, regularly issued under the authority of our Grand Lodge, aforesaid, to assemble as a regular Lodge, in the town of ———:

KNOW YE, That reposing special trust and confidence, in the talents and Masonic intelligence of our Worshipful Brother ——— ———, we have thought proper, ourselves being unable to attend, to constitute and appoint our said Worshipful Brother ——— ———, to constitute "IN FORM," the Brethren aforesaid, into a regular Lodge, to be known and distinguished by the name of ——— Lodge, No. —, and to install their officers elect, agreeably to ancient form and the customs of the Craft; and for so doing this shall be his warrant.

[SEAL] Given under our hands, and the seal of the Grand Lodge of ———, of Ancient, Free, and Accepted Masons, at ———, this ——— day of ———, A. D. ———, A. L. ———.

——— ———, *Grand Master.*

——— ———, *Grand Secretary.*

FORM OF COMMISSION FOR DISTRICT DEPUTY GRAND MASTERS.

[SEAL]
——— ———, G. M.

By virtue of the authority in me vested, I do, by these Presents, appoint the Right Worshipful ——— ———, of ———, to be District Deputy Grand Master for the ——— Masonic District in this Commonwealth, which District includes the several Lodges here mentioned, viz.

And he is hereby authorized, during the present year, ending the ——— day of ——— next, (unless this Commission should be sooner revoked by me,) to exercise all the duties, powers, and privileges thereof, agreeably to the Laws of the Grand Lodge aforesaid, and the ancient usages of Freemasons:

And it is hereby enjoined on him to watch over the interests of the Lodges aforesaid, with all due vigilance, as the true and faithful representative of the GRAND MASTER.

In testimony whereof, I have hereunto set my name, and caused the seal of the Grand Lodge aforesaid to be affixed, this ——— day of ———, Anno Domini one thousand eight hundred and ———, and of Masonry five thousand eight hundred and ———.

Attest, ——— ———, *Grand Secretary.*

FORM OF COMMISSION FOR RE-APPOINTMENT.

From the East of the Grand Lodge of ———.

This ——— day of ———, A. L. five thousand eight hundred and ———.
To all the Fraternity of Free and Accepted Masons whom it may concern:

   [SEAL] I do re-appoint for the present year of our Masonic
       Jurisdiction, (ending the ——— ——— day of ———
 —— ——, G. M. next,) our Right Worshipful Brother ——— ———
       District Deputy Grand Master, for the ——— Masonic
       District in this State, which District contains the following Lodges, viz.:

And hereby empower him to exercise all the duties, powers and privileges of said office of District Deputy Grand Master, agreeably to the Regulations of the GRAND LODGE, and for the benefit of the LODGES before mentioned, as particularly expressed in the Commission given him at his first appointment.

 Attest,   ——— ———, *Grand Secretary.*

FORM OF PROXY FOR REPRESENTATIVE IN GRAND LODGE.

To the Most Worshipful Grand Lodge of ———.

 BE IT KNOWN,

  [SEAL] That Brother ——— ———, of ———, having been chosen by
      the members of ——— Lodge, in ———, to represent said
——— ———, Lodge in Grand Lodge the ensuing year: I do, by these
Master of presents, in their behalf, constitute and appoint him their
——— *Lodge.* representative; for them to appear, and upon all subjects
      relating to the Craft in general, and to said Lodge in particular, to act and decide as fully as though we were personally present.

Confirming the acts of our beloved Brother, in his capacity aforesaid—We pray that he may enjoy all the privileges and protection to which we are entitled.

In witness whereof, I have hereunto subscribed my name, and caused the seal of our Lodge to be affixed, this ——— day of ———, A. L. 58—.

 Attest,

            ——— ———, *Secretary.*

THE

FREEMASONS' MONTHLY MAGAZINE,

PUBLISHED MONTHLY,

AT

21 SCHOOL STREET,

BOSTON.

CHARLES W. MOORE, Editor.

TERMS—TWO DOLLARS PER ANNUM.

THIS WORK IS EXCLUSIVELY DEVOTED TO THE DISCUSSION OF

Masonic Principles,

AND THE DIFFUSION OF

MASONIC INTELLIGENCE, FOREIGN AND DOMESTIC.

RECOMMENDATION.

In Masonic Convention,
Gr. Lodge Saloon, Baltimore, May 16, 1843.

Br. S. W. B. Carnegy, of Missouri, presented the following, which was unanimously adopted—

Resolved, That the interest of the Masonic Fraternity, and the good of mankind, may be greatly promoted by the publication of a periodical, devoted to Freemasonry. This Convention, therefore, cheerfully and earnestly recommend the "FREEMASONS' MONTHLY MAGAZINE," edited and published by Br. CHARLES W. MOORE, of Boston, Mass., as eminently useful and well deserving the generous patronage, support and study of the whole Fraternity.

Extract from the minutes.   ALBERT CASE,
Sec'y National Masonic Con.

(CIRCULAR)

A broadside written and circulated by Charles W. Moore, Grand Secretary of the Grand Lodge of Massachusetts, in defense of the publication of the *Trestle-Board*.

(CIRCULAR)

Boston, January 27, 1844.

R. W. Brother:—You have probably received from Br. John Dove, Grand Secretary of the Grand Lodge of Virginia, a "Circular," in reference to the new Trestle-Board, recently published by a majority of the Committee appointed by the late National Masonic Convention to prepare it.

The communication in question, is so unjustifiably abusive in its terms, that I should not condescend to notice it at all, and certainly not to trouble you with this hasty reply, were it not that entire silence, on my part, might be construed into a tacit admission of the truth of its misrepresentations.

By reference to the proceedings of the Convention, (p. 35) you will perceive, that I was chairman of the Committee, to whom the consideration of the subject of a Trestle-Board was originally referred by that body. The report, embracing a general outline of the work, was written by me, and signed by Brs. Delafield, and *Carnegy*. The views of the Committee were, so far as I understood them, that the work should partake of the general character of similar publications, except that it should be made more *practical* in its adaptation, and less voluminous and costly. The *omission* of the usual Illustrations, or Explanations, as contended for by Br. Dove, (and this is the source of the present difficulty,) was not, to my knowledge, either suggested or contemplated. *I would not have been engaged in preparing a* Text-Book *without them*; because I believe that such a book would be of no more use in the *practical operations* of the Lodge-room, than any of the old Ahiman Rezons; and because such a work is not, in my judgment, adapted to "reflect the true work" of the Convention, or to "take the place of all those works" (the Monitor, Chart, &c.) which Br. Dove has seen fit to denounce as "clumsy and spurious." I regard well adapted text-books as the *conservative agents* by which alone uniformity of work, in distant Lodges, can be preserved. They are so regarded by intelligent and well informed Brethren in all parts of the world. They have been in use in this country for more than a century, and in Europe for a much longer time. One of the best scholars in England, the Rev. Dr. OLIVER, and one of the most profound antiquaries in France, Mons. ROSENBERG, of Paris, have both recently been engaged, the former in re-editing, and the latter in producing works of this description, the fulness and clearness of the explanations of which are esteemed by our trans-atlantic Brethren as their great merit. The Trestle-Board is a sealed-book in comparison with them. Their authors are the most distinguished Masons living, whether regarded with reference to their general learning or their extensive acquaintance with the practical or archeological details of the Institution. My Br. Dove may be a wiser and more learned man than either of them, but I am not in possession of the evidence of the fact, and shall therefore continue, for the present at least, to regard them as preferable authority in all matters of a Masonic character.

The report above alluded to, having been adopted by the Convention, the preparation of the work was referred to a Committee, consisting of Brs. Dove, Carnegy and myself, with, I presume, the distinct understanding of every member of the Convention, that I was to prepare the work. This was perfectly well understood by the committee; and the business was put into my hands without any "full, frank and free interchange of ideas on the subject." Very little was at that time said in my presence about it. Brs. Dove and Carnegy had some conversation in relation to it, and were to give me their views in writing on their return home. I was then to act upon their advice, as my own judgment should dictate. *I was not to submit the work for the approval of Br. John Dove.* I entered into no such arrangement, nor was I under any different obligations to him than to Br. Carnegy. I entertained no such exalted opinion of the Masonic erudition, or of the correctness of the judgment of that Brother, as such an agreement would seem to imply.

Thus the matter stood until the 20th June, when, not hearing from Br. Dove, I addressed him on the subject. His answer is dated the 3d July. In it he says—"a small volume, say duodecimo, containing all the emblems of the Chart, in the three first Degrees, together with the ancient charges, the forms of ceremonies, prayers, &c., seems to be the book we need. To this I think may safely be added the emblems, &c. of the Degree of Past Master. * * * * * Let there be as little letter-press as possible, particularly concerning *explanation*, for *we* in Virginia have the greatest imaginable dread of printing Masonry." I have not a copy of my answer to this letter. I, however, objected to the exclusion of the *explanations* of the emblems, and I think expressed a desire to include in the work the Degrees conferred in the Chapters and Encampments,—a desire which I subsequently yielded to the ascertained wishes of the majority of the Committee.

The next letter I received from Br. Dove, is dated the 23d of August. In it he fully states his views of the character of the proposed work. I subjoin his description entire, and respectfully ask that you will take the work, *as published*, and compare it with the description here given, *by him*, and ascertain for yourself, wherein the one differs from the other.

"It was intended by us to shelf all other books upon the subject, and must inevitably have that effect if brought out in a style and form deserving the patronage of individual members; in order to do this the arrangement of hieroglyphics and emblems *cannot* materially vary from that to which the Fraternity have been accustomed, and which is best set forth in Parmly's or Cross' Charts, for this purpose I would recommend that you cause to be Lithographed *three entire floor cloths*, one for each Degree, a fac simile of which may be painted on a large scale, in oil cloth, to be used in the Lodge: and then somewhat in the order of Parmly, or Cross, arrange them for explanation in the order in which they will be made to appear in the Lecture, including the Past Master's Degree. So much for the picture part.

"I would simply DESCRIBE each Hyeroglyphic or emblem, and leave out all the speculative explanation, as for example, when *describing* the working tools of an E. A., I would say, "the twentyfour inch gauge is an instrument used by operative workmen to measure and lay off their work," or *words to that effect*, and then stop. "The common Gavel is an instrument used by operative Masons to break off the rough corners of stones, the better to fit them for the builder's use," and then stop, and *by no means* to say what we as speculative Masons do with them, &c. I would leave out all such words as "signs," "tokens," &c. Having finished the EXPLANATIONS I would insert all the ancient charges to a newly made Brother under the following heads—1. *God and Religion.* 2. *As a Citizen.* 3. *As a Mason in Lodge.* 4. *After Lodge and before dispersed.* 5. *When at home as to Masons.* 6. *When at home as a neighbor,* &c.; next what is called *the* charge in each Degree, the forms of prayer in each Degree, and those used at opening and closing, and in fine *every thing* proper to be written concerning the three Degrees.

"Under the head of Past Master's Degree I would then insert at length all the forms and ceremonies of Funerals, laying Corner Stones, Dedications, &c. &c., and this with a very few well selected songs should compose the *entire* book."

I might with safety leave the whole matter here—trusting to the result of the comparison I request, for an entire justification from the unmasonic abuse of Br. Dove. *The work is in almost exact correspondence with his own suggestions.* My reply, dated August 26, contained the following:—

"In preparing the 'hieroglyphics,' or emblems, I shall neither follow Cross nor Parmly. I shall not, however, change the character of any of them. With *this* part of the work you will be satisfied.

"Touching the Illustrations,—I propose to give them as they are contained in Webb, and, substantially, as they were published in England more than one hundred years ago—as they are contained in Preston—as they exist in France and all over the continent—and as you may find them in all the text-books on Masonry. *I can consent to no change in this respect.* We may be wiser than our fathers in some things, but in this I am satisfied with *their* wisdom. As to the use of the words 'signs,' 'tokens,' &c., I do not think I shall have occasion to use them, though I see no particular objection to doing so. I will, however, endeavor to avoid them.

"The charges you name, properly belong to the Book of Constitutions. I shall not, however, object to insert those under the heads of 'God and Religion,'—'as a Citizen,'—'On the behavior of Masons in Lodges,' &c.—'after Lodge,' &c., 'when at home,' &c., as you suggest. I have pursued the line you mark out in relation to the Past Master's Degree."

In this letter I again urged the insertion of what are called the higher degrees, but expressed a willingness to surrender the whole matter into the hands of Br. Dove. His reply was limited to an objection to the insertion of the degrees in question. This, as before remarked, I abandoned; and in doing so, supposed all difficulty was removed. I accordingly put the work to press, *on the plan suggested by Br. Dove in his letter of the 23d of August* —presuming that if I followed *his* advice, *he* at least would have no cause to complain. But to my surprise, I received a letter from him, dated the 26th September, informing me of the receipt of one from Br. Carnegy, in which he says, "there is not the *shadow of difference* between him (Carnegy) and myself," (Dove.) He then adds, "*your* views of the work do not coincide with *ours*." Never having had any other difference with Br. Carnegy than that in reference to the insertion of the higher degrees, and having yielded to him in that particular, the inference was, that if Br. Dove agreed with him, *all difference of opinion was reconciled;* and so it would have been, had Br. Dove told me the *truth*, in saying, "there was not the *shadow of difference* between him and Br. Carnegy." I will prove this directly, by letters from Br. Carnegy himself. I will add here, that Br. Dove had by this time *changed his mind* in respect to the "three entire floor cloths," spoken of in his letter of the 23d Aug., and come to the conclusion that the emblems should be dispersed "through the body of the book in order that it may act the part of a hieroglyphical monitor to each instructor." Why disperse them through the body of the book, if the explanations were to be omitted?

Presuming, from the tenor of his letter of the 23d August, that there was then no essential difference between us, I put the work to press, and had, on the receipt of his of 26th Sept., printed 48 pages,—including the whole of the first three degrees. These I immediately sent him, *in the firm conviction that they would receive his entire approval.* But to my astonishment, I received for answer that the work could not receive the sanction of his name! I had gone too far to recede, or I would have abandoned it. My plates were engraved, paper purchased, and printing nearly completed. I however suspended the work, and sent a copy (complete with the exception of the last ten pages) to Br. Carnegy, for his examination, with the determination to let the question of its publication, as the report of the committee, be settled by his decision of its merits. His answer is dated Oct. 30th, and from it I make the following extract:—

"*Palmyra, Mo., Oct.* 30th, 1843.

"My Dear Bro. Comp. and Friend.—Yours of 15th inst. was received yesterday—the information it contains has given me more pain of mind than any thing which has occurred in my past life. I shall write immediately to Br. Dove, and pray him to acquiesce in the use of his name to the Trestle-Board—and I wish you to delay as long as you can for an answer from him, as I hope to satisfy him that he should agree and sanction the work, and shall request him to write you on receipt of mine to him *

"For myself (after an examination of the Trestle-Board received with your letter) I approve of it, and authorize you to use my name in any manner you may deem proper. If it can be of any use affix it to such certificate, preface or circular as you deem proper to insert in the Book, and I hope it may be received by the Craft, with the same feelings of approval which I myself entertain for it. On the best comparison I can draw between it and the various Books intended for the like use, I am sure it is greatly better than any hitherto published. Indeed it cannot fail of universal acceptation. I had hoped that it would cost less than $9,† but you have doubtless done all you could to lesson its cost, and I am no judge of what it should be. Through Br. Singleton, I last week ordered one dozen copies for my Lodge, and doubt not but one thousand copies will be required for Missouri in less than one year. Before dismissing the subject of the Book, I should be allowed to say, *that it is very nearly in exact form and substance with that agreed upon before we separated*, and now that the proposition to insert the R. A. degrees is surrendered by you, I am not able to see any thing to which Br. Dove can in the least object, (except it be the plates), and them I positively required before we parted and his objections were not pressed. Now, on reading the quotations of his letter, I am sure there is not any thing contained or omitted which authorizes him to withhold the influence of his name. For myself I am delighted with the Book. *It is just what the Lodges need*, and I am gratified not a little in having aided (however small the help has been) in giving to the Masonic world a Book, which, unpretending in itself, cannot fail to become of greater benefit than *all* that have been previously published. I would write a review of it for the Magazine, but for the relation I bear to it."

Signed,   S. W. B. CARNEGY.

You will bear in mind that Br. Dove, in his letter of 26th Sept., says, "there is not the *shadow of* DIFFERENCE between Br.

---

* I accordingly delayed the work twenty days, and wrote Br. Dove myself, urging that as we had yielded to him in many respects, he was bound to yield to the will of the majority, in this wherein we still differed. I received no answer.

† The price was subsequently reduced to eight dollars a dozen, that there might not be any complaint on this score.

Carnegy and myself." Was he authorized to say this? That there may be no mistake in this matter,—for it places Br. Dove in an unenviable position,—I subjoin an extract of another letter from Br. Carnegy, dated Sept., 16th,—only *five days* after the date of his letter to Br. Dove,—in which he gives his views of what the character of the proposed work should be;—

"I wish the Book," he says, "to contain the emblems of the three first degrees, and the Past Master's degree,* after the manner of the Chart, only I would have them on a smaller scale, and would arrange them in the exact order in which they are to be used in instruction, and the *Illustrations* as used by *Webb* and *Cross*. I would arrange the scriptures, lectures, prayers, charges, and *illustrations*, as they occur in practice."

I have desired you to take the trouble to compare the Trestle-Board with the plan indicated by Br. Dove in his letter of 23d August, and I now make the same request in respect to the above, from Br. Carnegy. If I am not greatly mistaken, the result of such an examination will show that there was, *at one time*, an almost entire agreement between *all* the members of the Committee; and it will also show that the interruption of this unanimity and the breaking of the agreement, is attributable neither to Br. Carnegy nor myself.

As still further illustrative of Br. Carnegy's views, I give the following extract of a letter from him, dated Aug. 10th. He says:—

"In the notes or observations designed as directions as to the use of the several portions of the Book, I would be as *explicit as possible*, for we often consider others whom we seek to instruct, as already versed in many things of which they are really ignorant, and as able to comprehend instructions which need explanation."

This request was followed, and I presume the propriety of it will not be questioned by any intelligent Brother. In the same letter, in speaking of the ceremonies of installation, consecration, &c., he says—"They need revision. I wish you therefore to examine them with care and analyze every thought and every word, and so *alter, amend* and *strike out*, as that they shall appear

---

* The emblems of P. M. degree were omitted on account of expense.

perfect in sentiment and style." This advice was observed in respect to all parts of the work, so far as my time would permit. I would not consent to retain an unmeaning or objectionable sentence, or a piece of bad grammar, or false rhetoric, for no better reason than that it was written some fifty or sixty years ago. I have accordingly rewritten the charge to the first degree, and amended those of the 2d and 3d, where, in my judgment, it was required. This has been done, to some extent, by the authors of all the text books published since Br. Preston (by whom they were originally written,) first issued his "Illustrations of Masonry." The entered apprentice charge, as contained in the Trestle-Board, corresponds, almost precisely, with the charge at present used in English. I am unwilling to believe that the emendations to which I have alluded, or such others as have been made, will be regarded, by any well informed Brother, as constituting an objection to the work.†

All I ask of my Brethren is, that they institute the examination I have requested. They will find in the matter and arrangement of the work, an *almost precise correspondence* with the views of Br. Carnegy, as above expressed, and with those of the dissenting Brother, as contained in his letter of the 23d Aug. That my Br. Dove's opinion would not stand twenty-four hours, without changing, is the misfortune of his peculiar temperament —not my fault. In his gyrations I chose to take him at that point most favorable to what I conceived to be the wishes of the Convention. There I shall hold him. He may flutter, but cannot escape.

He says the TRESTLE-BOARD does not represent the work and lectures agreed upon by the Convention. If he had designed to be his own executioner, this was the weapon for him to make use of. And I must ask you again to refer to the printed proceedings of the Convention. You will there perceive that the more important portions of the reports of the Committee on Work were made to the Convention by me. The answers, if I recollect rightly, were given by me in all the degrees, except the first section of the third. The ceremonies of opening and closing were mainly rehearsed by Br. Dove. I refer to this fact merely for the purpose of showing that I probably understand what I reported, and what was adopted by the Convention, as well, at least, as the delegate from Virginia. Besides, I was engaged in

---

† The Convention did not order a *reprint* of the Monitor, but a *new work*.

qualifying members, while in Baltimore, after the adjournment of the Convention, and after Br. Dove had left for Virginia. I have also been engaged in imparting instruction to several of the delegates since my return to Boston, who have come from other States expressly for the information. Would they have done this, had they supposed I did not understand the work as agreed upon in the Convention? Were not they capable of judging?

Again. The work and lectures adopted, are the same, with a few verbal variations, as first taught in this country by the late R. W. Br. THOMAS SMITH WEBB, of Rhode Island, and which have been in use in this Commonwealth, and throughout New England, and, to some extent, though not always in their purity, in nearly every State in the Union, for the last forty years. They are the system on which I have practised for *twentytwo years*, and with it I am at least as familiar as the delegate from Virginia. I put it, then, to my Brethren, to say, whether they can believe for a moment, that I have produced a *text-book* not in conformity with the work of the Convention? My Br. Dove's malevolence was father to this thought.

But the matter does not stop here. That the TRESTLE-BOARD is correctly and precisely adapted to the system as taught by Br. Webb, I offer the testimony of R. W. Br. BENJ. GLEASON, Esq., who, in my opinion, has not, as a lecturer, a superior in the United States. He was a pupil of Br. Webb's in 1801, and has been almost constantly engaged in teaching the lectures since that period. He has taught in every State in the Union. Within the last five years he has spent months instructing Lodges and Brethren in *Virginia*. From him my Br. Dove has himself received instruction, and I may add, there is still room for him to draw from the same excellent fountain. Br. Gleason, in his recommendation attached to the work, says—"Wherefore, as a Brother, 'well instructed,' permit me, *without hesitation*, earnestly to recommend your good work, *as well calculated to facilitate the acquisition of the Lectures—to preserve the ceremonials and usages traditions and lectures, in their purity.*" I may be permitted to say, that Br. Gleason has been my teacher.

In addition to this, I likewise offer you the testimony of the venerable Br. JOHN B. HAMMATT, the present D. Grand Master of Massachusetts, Past District Deputy Grand Master of *Virginia*, and Past Dep. G. Master of the Dist. of Columbia. He is a working Freemason of *fortythree years* standing, and says— "I most cordially and unequivocally recommend the Trestle-

Board as being *more practical and better adapted to Lodge purposes*, than any other work which has fallen under my observation." I also give you the testimony of the Grand Officers, including the *Grand Lecturers*, of the Grand Lodge of this Commonwealth. They are practical, experienced, and competent Brethren. Their certificates are appended to the Trestle-Board, and to them I refer you.

I come now to another class of evidence, the competency of which cannot be questioned, and which I presume will be admitted to be conclusive as to the adaptation of the Trestle-Board to the work of the Convention. I mean the testimony of the members of the Convention themselves—each one of whom must be admitted to be as good a witness in the case, as Br. Dove, or the *"distinguished Brother."*‡ from the District of Columbia. The first I shall offer is the certificate of Rev. Br. CASE, Secretary of the Convention:

Charleston, S. C., Dec. 1843.

R. W. Br. MOORE,—I have received and carefully examined the new "MASONIC TRESTLE BOARD," prepared by yourself and P. G. M. Carnegy, in accordance with the will of the National Masonic Convention. I congratulate the Editors on the completion of their labors, and while I regret that the Committee were not entirely unanimous in presenting so invaluable a work, I assure you that, in my opinion, the "TRESTLE-BOARD" *is all the Convention desired it should be*—better than any other text-book for Masonic purposes, and that it will meet the approbation of the Convention, and the Fraternity. The omission suggested by the dissenting Brother, would much lessen the value of the work for general use. To the exoteric Mason the omission would be no disadvantage. But there are, and will be many of the esoteric school, who rule in Lodges, and to such, the illustrations are absolutely necessary. If the text-book did not contain them, the Master and Pupil would often be found far in the *North*, seeking knowledge in the dark.

I repeat—I believe the book is what the Convention desired; that it will be of infinite service in securing uniformity in the work of the Lodges, and that the intelligent craftsmen who have prepared it, will see their work approved, and be greeted by the Convention with "well done," faithful and true Brothers.

ALBERT CASE,
Sec. of the late Nat. Masonic Convention.

---

‡ I am not responsible for the *italic*—that belongs to Br. Dove or his Committee.

The following is a general Certificate authorized and bearing the names of *nine* members of the Convention. To these the names of the editors are to be added—making *eleven* of the *sixteen* members who composed the Convention. They stand opposed to the prejudiced testimony of Br. Dove, and that of the *"distinguished Brother,"* from the District of Columbia. The remaining *three* members of the Convention have not yet been heard from.

The undersigned, Members of the late National Masonic Convention, having examined the TRESTLE-BOARD, prepared by R. W. Brs. MOORE and CARNEGY, recommend it to the Fraternity throughout the United States, as a MANUAL, singularly well adapted to the purposes, for which its publication was ordered by the Convention. They believe it to be all the Convention designed it should be, and that its general use by the Lodges cannot fail to secure a great degree of uniformity in the Work and Lectures.

>ALBERT CASE, of South Carolina.
>JOHN H. WHEELER, of North Carolina.
>JOSEPH FOSTER, of Missouri.
>THOMAS CLAPHAM, of New-Hampshire.
>WILLIAM FIELD, of Rhode Island.
>DANIEL A. PIPER, of Maryland.
>THOMAS HAYWARD, of Florida.
>LEMUEL DWELLE, of Georgia.
>EDWARD HERNDON, of Alabama.

The following are extracts from letters received from the members of the Convention whose signatures they bear. They are all *decided* and *explicit* as to the merits of the work.—

Pawtucket, R. I. Dec. 23, 1843.

R. W. BR. MOORE—I have given the TRESTLE-BOARD a thorough examination; and highly approve of it, in all its parts: and I am perfectly willing you should use my name, as a member of the Convention, in recommending it to the Fraternity.

>WILLIAM FIELD.

City of Raleigh, December 22, 1843.

MY DEAR SIR—Yours of the 5th inst. arrived by due course of mail, and I have thus long delayed my answer, expecting daily the new TRESTLE BOARD,—which only arrived last night,—with which I am much pleased. It is just what the Craft needed, as a *vade mecum* for Lecturers, Masters and others, and will doubtless be the means of producing much good and uniform Work. You have free right to use my name to the *general recommendation*. I am, Fraternally, yours, JNO. H. WHEELER.

Gainesville, January 2, 1844.

R. W. BR. MOORE—Your kind favor of 6th Dec., accompanied with a copy of the new Masonic Trestle-Board, is duly at hand, for which please accept my thanks. I have given the Work a perusal and examination. It appears to be the very thing, and well adapted to the purposes for which it is designed. The pictorial plates exhibit at one glance all the emblems belonging to each Degree, and are well calculated to assist both the Master and candidate, and then the letter press explanation of each emblem, is concise and forcible—and must impress the mind of the candidate with their importance.

I unhesitatingly give my most hearty sanction to the work—and without flattery, give credit to Br. Carnegy and yourself, for the beautiful style with which it is got up. You are authorized to make such use of my name in recommending the work, as may best make for its interest. I would prefer a Certificate, under my own proper name as Grand Lecturer of Alabama, to be affixed to it, and you may make such Certificate, choosing the form and style; setting forth in the most ample manner my entire approval of the TRESTLE-BOARD.

Truly your friend and Brother,

EDWARD HERNDON.

Baltimore, December 28, 1843.

DEAR SIR AND BROTHER—I have received a copy of the TRESTLE-BOARD, as prepared by Br. Carnegy and yourself, and which you were kind enough to send me. I have examined it and it meets with my entire approval. I could have no objection to recommend it as Grand Lecturer of Maryland, but I think a **general** recommendation, signed by the members of the late Convention, would be preferable: however, as it is, in my judgment, the best arranged work I have seen, you are at liberty to use my name in any way you may think best, in recommendation of it.

Respectfully and Fraternally yours,

D. A. PIPER.

Augusta, Ga., January 9, 1844.

BR. MOORE—I cheerfully accord to you the use of my name, as a member of the Baltimore Convention, in recommending to the Fraternity of the United States, the "TRESTLE-BOARD," prepared by yourself and Bro. Carnegy, to be used as a manual or text-book throughout the Union. The examination of the work afforded me much satisfaction, and I most heartily congratulate you both upon the success attending your efforts in arranging and embodying in the Trestle-Board, (effectually as I conceive,) *the great object designed by the late National Masonic Convention*, and as such cordially recommend it.

Yours, very Respectfully,

LEMUEL DWELLE.

Tallahassee, Dec. 18, 1843.

R. W. BR. MOORE—Your letter of the 6th inst., with a copy of the Trestle-Board, reached me yesterday, and I have examined it through, and feel gratified at the manner in which you and Br. Carnegy have got it up.

I myself, as an individual member, give it my most cordial approval, and request you, if you see proper, to add my name among its advocates.

Respectfully your friend and Brother,

THOMAS HAYWARD.

In the belief that, if he be not wholly reckless, here is testimony enough to overwhelm the delegate from Virginia with shame and confusion, I will only add the official action of the Grand Lodges of Massachusetts, New Hampshire, and Rhode Island, and the Certificate of the Grand Officers of the Grand Lodge of South Carolina, and refer you to the Freemasons' Magazine for December last, for other testimony:—

FROM THE GRAND LODGE OF MASSACHUSETTS.

The Committee to whom were referred the doings of the Masonic Convention, held at Baltimore, having reported at a previous meeting of this Grand Lodge, on the topics then presented, are now enabled to complete their duties, by an expression of their opinions on the merits of the "TRESTLE-BOARD," which has been published within a few days.

This important work was prepared by R. W. CHARLES W. MOORE, of Massachusetts, and R. W. S. W. B. CARNEGY, of Missouri, the majority of the Committee to whom its preparation was referred.

The "Trestle-Board," prepared under such supervision, the Committee, without any distrust of their opinion, affirm, will meet the approbation of the Fraternity. Even the expunging of what was wholly "irrelevant and useless" in the former Text-Books, will be of great utility. Claims questionable in their nature, and assertions founded on at least equivocal authority, have too long occupied the pages of our "hand-books" of Masonry. Inflated and exaggerated statements only serve to retard the progress of institutions. "Absurd and ridiculous pretentions are no more justifiable in societies than individuals. Freemasonry requires only what fairly and honestly belongs to it;" and your Committee anticipate, that this MANUAL, in its beautiful simplicity, will do much to commend our much loved association to the favorable estimation of all who peruse it.

It would not be within the province of the Committee to enter into an analysis of the work, or to present a review of its arrangement, literary character, &c. But that it will stand the test of criticism in this particular, they have no misgivings.

Their duty will be accomplished by reporting to this Grand Lodge, for their approval, the following Resolution:

Resolved, That the Grand Lodge of Massachusetts recommend the "Trestle-Board" prepared by a Committee of the late National Convention, as a work embodying all the essentials of a Manual of Ancient Craft Masonry; and in preference to all other similar works, it especially sanctions to the subordinate Lodges under this jurisdiction, the use of this most excellent compend of the principles and ceremonials of the Order.

> WINSLOW LEWIS, JR.
> JOHN B. HAMMATT,
> E. M. P. WELLS,
> JOHN R. BRADFORD,
> HUGH H. TUTTLE,
> *Committee.*

[Adopted in Grand Lodge, Dec. 13, 1843.]

FROM THE GRAND LODGE OF NEW HAMPSHIRE.

At a communication of the M. W. Grand Lodge of New

Hampshire, held at Portsmouth, Dec. 13, A. L. 5843, the following resolution was adopted, viz:

Resolved, By the M. W. Grand Lodge of New Hampshire, that the "MASONIC TRESTLE-BOARD" by R. W. Brothers Charles W. Moore and S. W. B. Carnegy, adapted to the National System of Work and Lectures as revised and perfected by the late U. S. Masonic Convention, be, and the same is hereby approved; and it is hereby ordered, that the same be used by the several Lodges under this jurisdiction, as a guide and text book in their labors.

     Attest,   ISAAC L. FOLSOM, *G. Sec.*

GRAND LODGE OF RHODE ISLAND.

The committee on the printed proceedings of the doings of the National Masonic Convention presented in their report the following on the Trestle-Board.

The Convention appointed "a committee to prepare and publish a text-book, to be called the Masonic Trestle-Board, which work is now completed agreeably to the rules and designs laid down by the Convention. A copy of the same has been examined by your committee, which has their cordial approbation, and it is earnestly recommended to this Grand Lodge for their approval, as a text book worthy the patronage of the Fraternity.

Which recommendation was adopted.

    Attest,

    JAMES HUTCHISON, *G. Secretary.*

FROM THE GRAND OFFICERS OF SOUTH CAROLINA.

We, the subscribers, officers of the M. W. Grand Lodge of South Carolina, have examined the "Masonic Trestle-Board," which has been just published by Brothers Moore and Carnegy, under the direction of the late National Masonic Convention, and we cheerfully recommend it to the patronage of the Fraternity. Masters of Lodges will find it of invaluable service while superintending the labors of the workmen, and to every Brother who seeks an increase of light it will afford important assistance. It is ornamented with the three "carpets," which are tastefully executed; that of the F. C. in particular is of an entirely original and very beautiful design. We therefore cordially unite with our Brethren of the Grand Lodge of Massachusetts in giving to it the sanction of our names.

Geo. B. Eckhard, M. W. G. Master; James C. Norris, Deputy Grand Master; John B. Irving, M. D., Senior Grand Warden; W. S. King, Junior Grand Warden; Albert Case, Grand Chaplain; John H. Honour, Grand Treasurer; A. G. Mackey, M. D. Grand Secretary; M. W. Henry A. Desaussure, P. G. Master; R. W. Wm. B. Foster, P. D. G. Master.

There is one infallible *test* by which the truth of the calumnious charge preferred by Br. Dove, may be tried by any skilful Brother. The system adopted by the Convention prevails, to a greater or less extent, in its outline and general features, in every State in the Union; and the Delegates to the Convention have probably made their reports to their respective Grand Lodges. Now, let any Brother, who is acquainted with the system as taught by Webb, Gleason, or Cross, *take the Trestle-Board in his hand and apply it to the work and lectures.* This will be a *practical test,* and will prove to a demonstration that it is *not only more distinct and explicit in its directions, but is better adapted to the purposes for which it is designed, than any other text-book hitherto published in this country.* This would not, I grant, come with a very good grace from me, if it were not amply sustained by the testimony of others,—including more than *two-thirds* of the members of the Convention.

I am admonished, by the sheets of manuscript before me, that I am extending my remarks to an inconvenient length, and that it will be impossible for me to notice, in detail, all the various misrepresentation contained in Br. Dove's "Circular," without quite exhausting your patience. Neither have I room to argue the case. I leave the naked testimony, therefore, to the good sense of my Brethren. To their decision, whatever it may be, I shall cheerfully submit. Br. Carnegy may think proper to address you on the subject; but of that I am not authorised to speak. I have had no consultation with him, and answer only for myself. A few words more, and I have done.

It will be seen by reference to the report of Br. Dove, as submitted to the Grand Lodge of Virginia, that he denounces all the text books which have, from time to time, been given to the Fraternity, as *"clumsy and spurious publications."* In this general denunciation is included Webb's Monitor. It is not, therefore, surprising that he should condemn the Trestle Board. To Br. Thomas Smith Webb and his Monitor are the Fraternity in this country more indebted for the beautiful lectures and work which now generally prevail, than to any other Mason who ever lived. This esteemed Brother and his Book,—for they are identical,—the Grand Secretary of Virginia denounces as *"clumsy and spurious!"* It remains to be seen whether the Fraternity will sanction the calumny,—heaped as it is upon the memory and the work of one who spent his life in the cause of Masonry. The Monitor spurious! My Br. Dove's acquaintance with Masonic literature may extend beyond the Virginia "Ahiman Rezon,"—a republican of which he would have forced upon the Fraternity as a TEXT-BOOK, could he have coaxed the majority of the Committee into a compliance with his schemes, —but he is not authorized to denounce the Masonic Work of Thomas Smith Webb, as "spurious," until he has given better evidence than is yet manifest, of his fitness to sit in judgment on the labors of the living.

Br. Dove speaks of "imprudent phraseology." I cannot consent to consult the views of that Brother in this respect. *Twenty years* experience as the editor of Masonic publications and a pretty thorough acquaintance with Masonic literature, afford me a better and safer guide. The Trestle-Board is cautiously guarded, and had Br. Dove been moderately conversant with the standard works of like character, he would not have ventured the remark. But he seems to have started with the determination to supply all deficiencies, in this respect, with sweeping denunciation.

He charges me with bad faith. This I return to him. My *interest* required that I should *agree* with him. What motive had I to act in bad faith? None whatever. Not so with him. He wished to carry a point—to bring the work out according to a standard of his own—or rather according to a standard which has been once tried in Virginia, and *failed.** He, therefore, encouraged me to proceed, until I had incurred a heavy expense

---

* The standard referred to, is the "Ahiman Rezon," republished, some forty years since, by a Br. John K. Read, and adopted by the Grand Lodge of Virginia as a *text-book*. It was not adapted to such purpose, and, of course failed of its object. If I am correctly informed, it threw the Lodges into irregularities, or perhaps I should say, they soon run into irregularities for want of a proper guide. The Grand Lodge discovered this, and afterwards sanctioned the *emblems* as published by Cross, but rejected his letter press *illustrations*. This, in the opinion of my Br. Dove, was the acme of perfection! And such a work— the "Ahiman Rezon" with *emblems!*—he would have forced upon the Committee if he could.

in engravings, and made all other arrangements for publishing the work. Then, thinking I would rather sacrifice my views than bring the work out without the sanction of his name, he turned his back upon himself. Here was *bad faith* and a motive for it. He failed in his object, and hence his vindictiveness.

The only "glaring fault and serious objection to the Trestle-Board," noticed by the Working Committee of the Grand Lodge of Virginia, is, that it comes well recommended—or in their own words, that it is recommended by "Brothers not members of the Grand Convention!" This they regard as an insult, and condemn the work! I am content to let it stand at that. That they could find no other objection, is a sufficient recommendation from that quarter.

That the Grand Lodge of Virginia would withhold its sanction of the work, was expected. I knew the pertinacity of Br. Dove's character too well to anticipate a different result. A *majority* of the Committee were opposed to his crude and infeasible notions, and *eleven-sixteenths* of the members of the Convention have declared *against* him, and in favor of the Work. But all this, in certain quarters, goes for nothing against his *ipse dixit*. The testimony of the most competent Masons in the country, is as dust in the balance, when placed against the mandate of one, who, but for the adventitious circumstance of having, in compliment to his age, been made President of the Baltimore Convention, would scarcely have been heard of beyond the limits of his own State. "Once a King always a King"—and now, forsooth, he must continue to wear the crown and wield the sceptre or there shall be no peace,—no union of action,—neither shall there be any rulers in Israel! I will submit to no such folly and presumption. In doing so, the Grand Lodge of Virginia has permitted herself to be placed in a false position, for which, I shall be greatly mistaken, if she do not hereafter hold her recording officer to a strict accountability.

I shall not probably consider myself called upon to notice further any thing which the Brother from Virginia may think proper to circulate. His conduct in the matter has been such as to forfeit all claim which he might otherwise have upon my attention.

The TRESTLE-BOARD is before the Fraternity. *It is the Work ordered by the Convention. It corresponds with the Work and Lectures agreed upon and adopted by that body.* THIS IS PROVED

BY THE TESTIMONY OF ELEVEN UNIMPEACHEABLE WITNESSES. It is denied by Brother *John Dove*.

    I am, Respectfully and Fraternally,

        Your friend and Brother,

            CHARLES W. MOORE.

Colophon

Trestle-Board

Twelve hundred copies of this limited edition were manufactured by Pantagraph Printing Company, and Bloomington Offset Process, Inc., of Bloomington, Illinois, the former doing the composition and binding, and the latter the presswork.

The type faces used are of the Linotype Janson and Monotype Garamond families. The facsimile pages were reproduced from a first edition of "Trestle-Board", now in the Library of the Grand Lodge of Massachusetts, who also furnished the copy of the "Circular" set in type.

The text paper is sixty pound basis Oldestyle, manufactured by the S. D. Warren Company. The book covers are made of Columbia Mills' Riverside Vellum over board and stamped in gold.

All volumes of The Masonic Book Club series are designed and prepared by Louis L. Williams, Alphonse Cerza, and Fred A. Dolan.

Related Titles from Westphalia Press

Ancient Mysteries and Modern Masonry: The Collected Writings of Jewel P. Lightfoot, Edited by Billy J. Hamilton Jr.

Jewel P. Lightfoot. Former Attorney General of the State of Texas. Past Grand Master of the Masonic Grand Lodge of Texas. From humble beginnings in rural Arkansas, he worked to become an educated man who excelled in law and Freemasonry. He was a gentleman of his time, well-known as a scholar, public speaker, and Masonic philosopher.

Essay on The Mysteries and the True Object of The Brotherhood of Freemasons
by Jason Williams

This isn't a reprint of a classic. It's a new rendition with new life breathed into it, to be enjoyed both by the layperson trying to understand the Craft and Masonic scholars taking a deeper dive into the fraternity's golden years—when the concepts of liberty and equality were still fresh.

Female Emancipation and Masonic Membership: An Essential Collection
By Guillermo De Los Reyes Heredia

Female Emancipation and Masonic Membership: An Essential Combination is a collection of essays on Freemasonry and gender that promotes a transatlantic discussion of the study of the history of women and Freemasonry and their contribution in different countries.

Freemasonry, Heir to the Enlightenment
by Cécile Révauger

Modern Freemasonry may have mythical roots in Solomon's time but is really the heir to the Enlightenment. Ever since the early eighteenth century freemasons have endeavored to convey the values of the Enlightenment in the cultural, political and religious fields, in Europe, the American colonies and the emerging United States.

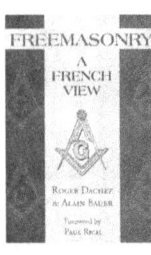

Freemasonry: A French View
by Roger Dachez and Alain Bauer

Perhaps one should speak not of Freemasonry but of Freemasonries in the plural. In each country Masonic historiography has developed uniqueness. Two of the best known French Masonic scholars present their own view of the worldwide evolution and challenging mysteries of the fraternity over the centuries.

Worlds of Print: The Moral Imagination of an Informed Citizenry, 1734 to 1839
by John Slifko

John Slifko argues that freemasonry was representative and played an important role in a larger cultural transformation of literacy and helped articulate the moral imagination of an informed democratic citizenry via fast emerging worlds of print.

Why Thirty-Three?: Searching for Masonic Origins
by S. Brent Morris, PhD

What "high degrees" were in the United States before 1830? What were the activities of the Order of the Royal Secret, the precursor of the Scottish Rite? A complex organization with a lengthy pedigree like Freemasonry has many basic foundational questions waiting to be answered, and that's what this book does: answers questions.

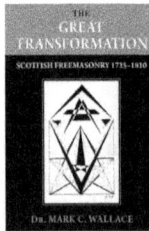

The Great Transformation: Scottish Freemasonry 1725-1810
by Dr. Mark C. Wallace

This book examines Scottish Freemasonry in its wider British and European contexts between the years 1725 and 1810. The Enlightenment effectively crafted the modern mason and propelled Freemasonry into a new era marked by growing membership and the creation of the Grand Lodge of Scotland.

Getting the Third Degree: Fraternalism, Freemasonry and History
Edited by Guillermo De Los Reyes and Paul Rich

As this engaging collection demonstrates, the doors being opened on the subject range from art history to political science to anthropology, as well as gender studies, sociology and more. The organizations discussed may insist on secrecy, but the research into them belies that.

A Place in the Lodge: Dr. Rob Morris, Freemasonry and the Order of the Eastern Star
by Nancy Stearns Theiss, PhD

Ridiculed as "petticoat masonry," critics of the Order of the Eastern Star did not deter Rob Morris' goal to establish a Masonic organization that included women as members. Morris carried the ideals of Freemasonry through a despairing time of American history.

Brought to Light: The Mysterious George Washington Masonic Cave
by Jason Williams MD

The George Washington Masonic Cave near Charles Town, West Virginia, contains a signature carving of George Washington dated 1748. This book painstakingly pieces together the chronicled events and real estate archives related to the cavern in order to sort out fact from fiction.

Dudley Wright: Writer, Truthseeker & Freemason
by John Belton

Dudley Wright (1868-1950) was an Englishman and professional journalist who took a universalist approach to the various great Truths of Life. He travelled though many religions in his life and wrote about them all, but was probably most at home with Islam.

History of the Grand Orient of Italy
Emanuela Locci, Editor

No book in Masonic literature upon the history of Italian Freemasonry has been edited in English up to now. This work consists of eight studies, covering a span from the Eighteenth Century to the end of the WWII, tracing through the story, the events and pursuits related to the Grand Orient of Italy.

westphaliapress.org

Policy Studies Organization

The Policy Studies Organization (PSO) is a publisher of academic journals and book series, sponsor of conferences, and producer of programs.

Policy Studies Organization publishes dozens of journals on a range of topics, such as European Policy Analysis, Journal of Elder Studies, Indian Politics & Polity, Journal of Critical Infrastructure Policy, and Popular Culture Review.

Additionally, Policy Studies Organization hosts numerous conferences. These conferences include the Middle East Dialogue, Space Education and Strategic Applications Conference, International Criminology Conference, Dupont Summit on Science, Technology and Environmental Policy, World Conference on Fraternalism, Freemasonry and History, and the Internet Policy & Politics Conference.

For more information on these projects, access videos of past events, and upcoming events, please visit us at:

www.ipsonet.org

www.ingramcontent.com/pod-product-compliance
Lightning Source LLC
Chambersburg PA
CBHW071714020426
42333CB00017B/2272